George Eugène-Fasnacht

Eugène's French method

Elementary French lessons

George Eugène-Fasnacht

Eugène's French method
Elementary French lessons

ISBN/EAN: 9783337281212

Printed in Europe, USA, Canada, Australia, Japan

Cover: Foto ©Paul-Georg Meister /pixelio.de

More available books at **www.hansebooks.com**

EUGENE'S
FRENCH METHOD
OR
ELEMENTARY FRENCH LESSONS

BEING A COURSE OF EASY RULES AND EXERCISES
INTRODUCTORY TO THE AUTHOR'S

"STUDENT'S COMPARATIVE FRENCH GRAMMAR."

TENTH EDITION.

THOROUGHLY REVISED.

By G. EUGENE-FASNACHT,
Assistant Master, Westminster School.

WILLIAMS & NORGATE,
14, HENRIETTA STREET, COVENT GARDEN, LONDON;
AND 20, SOUTH FREDERICK STREET, EDINBURGH.
1889.

PREFACE.

This Elementary Course of French Lessons is founded on Ahn's well known and well tried synthetical method. It differs, however, from Ahn's original work and from the host of its imitations in a few important distinctive features: —

The difficulties of pronunciation (and not only those of Grammar) are graduated — the first and second Exercises, for instance, containing only words with simple vowels; Ex. 3—6, words with accented vowels; Ex. 9—12, words with diphthongs; Ex. 13 and 14 words with nasal sounds — etc.;

The Conjugation of Verbs is introduced almost from the outset (Ex. 21), and continued to the end of the book; so that a pupil who has gone carefully through the work will have acquired a sound knowledge of the regular grammatical forms, and will thus be prepared to enter upon the systematic study of the advanced Grammar;

The Exercises are headed by easy Rules and practical Illustrations which set forth in strong contrast the differences of idiom and construction in the two languages, (see, for example, Ex. 31, 37, 83, 125—129, 145—148, etc.)

And last, but not least, the greatest care has been taken in the selection of type, to adapt the book, in this important but hitherto sadly disregarded point, to the wants of beginners. If this little work offered no other improvement, it would bear on every page its own justification for appearing in print.

TABLE OF CONTENTS.

(In Grammatical Order.)

NB. The numbers refer to the Exercises.

PRONUNCIATION:— Simple vowels, 1; Accented vowels, 3, 5; Diphthongs, 9, 11; Nasal sounds, 13; Final consonants, Liaison, 17; c, 19; g, 21; s, 27; h, 31; -ill-, -il, 69; -gn, 71; -ti, 73.

ARTICLE:— Definite, 1; l', 7; Plural, 23; Declined, 49; Partitive, 101, 105; Indefinite, 13.

SUBSTANTIVE: — Regular Formation of Plur., 23, 25; Plur. in x, aux, 95, 97; Irreg. Plur. 99; Declined 43—49; Partitive Gen. 101—105.

ADJECTIVE:— Possessive, 13, 15, 25; Demonstrative, 23; Formation of Plural, 23, 25, 59; Comparison, 89, 91; Regular Feminine, 29; Adj. in f and x, 39; Adj. in eil, el, en, on, er, 41; Adj. of three terminations, 107; Irreg. Fem., 109.

NUMERALS:— Cardinal, 51, 57; Ordinal, 75.

PRONOUNS:— Possessive, 83; Personal, 115—119, 125—129; en, 121; y, 123; Disjunctive Pers. Pron., 151; Relative 143; Demonstr., 145—148.

VERBS:— Avoir, Pres., 21, 35, 37; Indefinite 45; Imperf., 53; Preterite, 61; Future, 63; Conditional, 67; Imperat., 73; Future Past 77; Conditional Past, 79; Subjunctive Pres. & Imperf Subjunctive Perf. & Pluperf., 159.

TABLE OF CONTENTS.

VERBS:— Être, Pres., 27, 33, 35; Indefinite, 45; Imperf. 55; Preterite, 61; Future, 65; Condit., 67; Imperative, 73; Future Past 77; Condit. Past, 79; Subj. Pres. & Imperf., 157; Subj. Perf. & Pluperf., 159.

First Conjugation: **Parler**, Pres. & Imperat., 81; Imperf., 85; Preterite, 87; Future & Condit., 111; Compound Tenses, 113.

Second Conj.: **Finir**, 131, 133; Third Conj.: **Recevoir**, 135; Fourth Conj.: **Vendre**, 137, 139;

Conjugation of a Verb with être, 141; Passive Voice, 149; Reflect. Verb, 153; Impersonal Verb, 155; Sequence of Tenses, 159; Subjunctive of the four regular Conjugations, 161, 163.

ADVERBS:— Formation and Comparison of Adverbs, 93; Adverbs of Quantity, 103.

APPENDIX:— Formation of Tenses, p. 94; The four regular Conjugations, p. 96—103; Passive Voice, p. 106; Reflective Verb, p. 108.

READINGS:—

	page		page
L'Arabe et son cheval	110	Le Montagnard émigré.	113
Mieux que ça . . .	111	Le rat de ville et le rat	
Petit Pierre	113	des champs	114

VOCABULARY:— English-French, p. 116; to the Reading Lessons, p. 125.

The Alphabet.

Name:—
A, B, C, D, E, F, G, H, I, J, K, L, M,
ah, bay, say, day, ay, f, zhay, ash, ee, zhee, kah, l, m,
N, O, P, Q, R, S, T, U, V, X, Y, Z.
n, o, pay, küh, airr, s, tay, ü, vay, eex, eegrek, z.

1.

VOWELS.

a:— la, ma, ta, mal, lac, par, canal, fatal, parla;
i:— il, mil, fil, midi, fini, parti, ami;
e (mute):— le, me, te, ne; rare, barbe, dire, dame;
e (sound.):— bec, sec, miel, sel, Alfred, elle;
o:— or, rose, coq, sol, total, sorti, parole;
u:— lu, bu, su, vu, perdu, rue, une, lune, culture;
y:— tyrannic, pyramide, lyre, Tyr.

le, *the,* stands before **Masculine** nouns in the Singular:— le coq,
la, *the,* stands before **Feminine** nouns in the Sing.:— la lune.

There *is* no **Neuter** *gender* in *French.* All *nouns are either* **Masculine** *or* **Feminine**

la rose, *the rose*
le canif, *the penknife*
le mur, *the wall*
la lune, *the moon*
le coq, *the cock*
vu, *seen*

fini, *finished*
malade *ill, sick*
midi, *twelve o'clock* (*noon*)
il, *he, it*
elle, *she* (*it*)
a, *has*

est, (st *mute*) *is*
il a, *he has*
elle a, *she has*
il est, *he is*
elle est, *she is*
sur, *on, upon.*

1. Il a la rose. 2. Alfred a le canif. 3. Elle a vu la lune. 4. Le coq est sur le mur. 5. Il est malade. 6. Elle a le canif. 7. Il est midi. 8. Elle a fini. 9. Elle a vu la rose.

2.

1. Alfred has the rose. 2. He has the penknife. 3. She has seen the cock. 4. He is on the wall. 5. He has seen the moon. 6. She is ill. 7. He has finished. 8. It is twelve o'clock. 9. She has the rose.

3.
ACCENTED VOWELS.

é (e with an acute accent, *accent aigu*) called e fermé

dé, été, blé, vérité, donné, école.

    Obs. The terminations -ez, -ed, (also -er in words of more than one syllable) have the same sound as é (e fermé): as, donner, papier, pied, avez, nez, nier.

è (e with a grave accent, *accent grave*) \
ê (e with a circumflex, *accent circonflexe*) } called e ouvert (open e)

père, mère, frère, sévère, très, après, modèle; \
fête, tête, même, être, fenêtre, prêt.

    Obs. The termination -es, (also e in -er) in words of one syllable is pronounced like e ouvert: as, les, mes, tes, ses, ces; fer, mer.

le père, *the father*	parlé, *spoken*
le frère, *the brother*	fermé, *shut, closed*
la mère, *the mother*	donné, *given*
le fer, *the iron*	lu, *read*
la fenêtre, *the window*	fidèle, *faithful*
la porte, *the door, gate*	prêt, *ready*
le livre, *the book*	et (t always silent) *and*
le thé (th=t), *the tea*	dur, *hard*
apporté, *brought*	à, *to, at*.

1. Le père a parlé. 2. Le frère est fidèle. 3. Il a fermé la porte. 4. La mère a vu le frère. 5. Le frère a lu la lettre et le livre. 6. Le thé est prêt. 7. La mère a fermé la fenêtre. 8. Alfred a donné le livre à la mère. 9. Le père est malade. 10. Elle a fini le livre.

4.

1. The mother has spoken. 2. The father has read the letter. 3. (The) iron is hard. 4. The mother is faithful. 5. It is ready. 6. The brother has the book. 7. The father has shut the door. 8. He has shut the window. 9. The brother is ill. 10. She has given the letter to the mother.

5.

â, à (like a in *palm*):— pâle, âme, âne, mâle, blâme, là;
a (like a in *bark*):— il parle, ami, finira, capital;
ô (like o in *hope*):— trône, pôle, le nôtre, le vôtre;
o (like o in *hot*):— comédie, école, notre, votre, parole, poli;
o (*sonorous*):— or, il adore, il honore, cor, il dort (t mute).

le métal, *the metal*   honoré, *honoured*   pâle, *pale*
la patrie, *the native country* parti, *departed* perdu, *lost*
la dame, *the lady*   blâmé, *blamed*   poli, *polite, polished*
sorti, *gone out*   superbe, *splendid*   notre, *our*
la lecture, *the reading*   timide, *timid, shy*   votre, *your*.

1. Il a fermé la porte. 2. Votre ami est parti. 3. Il a parlé à la mère. 4. Elle a fini la lecture. 5. Le métal est poli. 6. Le livre est superbe. 7. Elle a honoré la mère. 8. Votre père est sorti. 9. La dame est pâle. 10. Elle a fermé la porte et la fenêtre.

6.

1. The moon is pale. 2. He has honoured the country. 3. Our father has (is) departed. 4. Your brother is shy. 5. He has blamed our brother. 6. Our father has spoken to your mother. 7. Your mother has given the letter to our brother. 8. The lady has lost the book. 9. The father is gone out. 10. Your brother has finished the reading.

7.

l' *stands instead of* le *or* la *before a word beginning with a* vowel *or* silent h:—

l'ami   *instead of* le ami,   *the friend.*
l'homme   *instead of* le homme,   *the man.*
l'âme   *instead of* la âme,   *the soul.*
l'habitude   *instead of* la habitude, *the habit.*

l'étude, *f. the study*   l'été, *m. the summer*   la pomme, *the apple*
l'or, *m. the gold*   l'herbe, *f. the grass*   mortel, *mortal*
l'homme, *m. the man*   l'âne, *m. the ass*   rare, *rare*
l'habit, *m. the coat*   le sable, *the sand*   facile, *easy*
l'arbre, *m. the tree*   la fable, *the fable*   sec, *dry*
l'animal, *m. the animal*   dormi, *slept*   bu, *drunk*.

1. L'étude est facile. 2. Il a lu la fable. 3. Emilie est pâle. 4. L'or est rare. 5. L'ami est fidèle. 6. L'homme est mortel. 7. L'habit est superbe. 8. La pomme est sur l'arbre. 9. L'été est sec. 10. L'âne est timide. 11. L'animal a dormi.

1*

8.

1. The cock is on the tree. 2. The friend has the coat. 3. The man is our brother. 4. The coat is ready. 5. She has given the grass to the animal. 6. The man is pale, he is ill. 7. The summer is splendid. 8. Our friend has the gold. 9. He has given the grass to the donkey. 10. Your friend has departed. 11. She has read the fable, it (she) is easy. 12. Our sister is timid.

9.

DIPHTHONGS.

ai, ei, (ais, ait, ay) *are pronounced like* è (e ouvert): *as,* mai, mais, le palais, la laine, l'aide, faire, clair, il plaît la reine, la peine, Madeleine, la Seine, la baleine.

But ai *is pronounced like* é (*e fermé*) *in the endings of Verbs* (*Preterite and Future*): *as,*

je donnai, je parlerai, *pronounce* donné, parleré.

au, eau, *are pronounced like* ô: *as,* le marteau, l'eau, beau, le tableau, le bateau, l'aune, l'autre; il aura, l'aurore, l'autel, la beauté.

le bateau, *the boat*
l'eau, *f. the water*
le palais, *the palace*
le gâteau, *the cake*
le tableau, *the picture*
la reine, *the queen*
le marteau, *the hammer*

l'autel, *m. the altar*
le vaisseau, *the ship*
le maître, *the master*
le roc, *the rock*
beau, *beautiful, fine*
frappé, *struck*
admiré, *admired*.

Obs. *Substantives ending in a diphthong are Masculine;* l'eau, *f., is an Exception.*

1. Le bateau est sur l'eau. 2. Le palais est beau. 3. Il a donné le gâteau à l'ami. 4. Le marteau a frappé le fer. 5. Votre ami a admiré le tableau. 6. Madeleine a vu la reine. 7. L'autel est superbe. 8. Le vaisseau est parti. 9. Le roc est dur. 10. La lecture est facile.

10.

1. He has seen the vessel on the Seine. 2. The man has lost the hammer. 3. The master has admired the palace. 4. The ship is on the rock. 5. The palace is magnificent. 6. The picture is on the wall. 7. Your mother has given the cake to Paul. 8. The queen has admired the picture. 9. Your ship has (is) departed. 10. It is on the water.

11.
DIPHTHONGS (continued).

eu, œu :— le feu, peu, le lieu, bleu ; neuf, seul, le bœuf, l'œuf ; la peur, la fleur, leur, le docteur, le cœur, le beurre.

oi :— le roi, la loi, la foi, moi, toi, l'étoile, la soif ; noir, la poire, le miroir, le soir.

ou :— ou, oui, le clou, le trou, trouvé, loué, la route ; pour, la tour, l'amour.

ui :— lui, l'huile, la tuile, la ruine, la pluie, fuir.

le feu, *the fire*
l'œuf, *m. the egg*
le roi, *the king*
la fleur, *the flower*
l'oiseau, *masc. the bird*
la poire, *the pear*
le voile, *the veil*
la voile, *the sail*
l'étoile, *f. the star*
le lac, *the lake*
le docteur, *the physician*
le malade, *the patient*
la sœur, *the sister*
le couteau, *the knife*
le beurre, *the butter*
clair, *clear*
bleu, *blue*
neuf, *new*
trouvé, *found*
loué, *praised*
fui, *fled*
pour, *for*.

Obs. *Names of fruits and flowers are feminine.*

1. Le feu est clair. 2. Le lac est bleu. 3. L'œuf est dur. 4. Le docteur a vu le malade. 5. Le roi a donné la fleur à la reine. 6. L'oiseau est sur l'arbre. 7. Louise a trouvé la poire. 8. Louis a vu l'étoile. 9. Le couteau est neuf. 10. L'oiseau a fui. 11. Votre sœur a le voile. 12. La voile est sur le vaisseau.

12.

1. The doctor has seen the king. 2. Your father has praised our friend. 3. Our sister has brought the knife for your friend. 4. The butter is for Louisa. 5. The pear is for your mother, and the egg is for your sister. 6. The bird has fled. 7. Your brother has found the boat and the sail. 8. Our sister has lost the veil. 9. Our friend has the flower. 10. Our bird is blue. 11. She has found your knife. 12. It is new.

13.
NASAL SOUNDS.

1. an, am, en, em :— le plan, Milan, Adam, la tante, la lampe, encore, le temple, la tente, l'empire.

2. ain, aim, in, im, ein, ien :— sain, le pain, la main, la faim, la fin, impur ; le sein, plein ; le mien, le tien, le sien.

3. on, om :— mon, ton, son, nom, ombre, le ballon, le monde.

4. un, um, eun :— un, lundi, aucun, brun, le parfum, à jeun.

NASAL SOUNDS.

These sounds are not nasal when followed by a vowel, or when m *or* n *is double: thus,*

Nasal	not Nasal	Nasal	not Nasal
l'an,	l'âne,	infidèle, impoli,	inutile, image,
le Romain,	la Romaine,	incivil,	innocent,
le lion,	la lionne,	loin,	le moine,
fin, le cousin,	fine, la cousine,	un,	une, la lune.

un, *a, an, one*
mon, *my* } *stand before* **Masculine** *nouns, singular:*
ton, *thy*
son, *his, her*

une, *a, an, one*
ma, *my* } *stand before* **Feminine** *nouns, singular,*
ta, *thy*
sa, *his, her*

as,

un roi,	a *king*	une reine,	a *queen*
mon frère	my *brother*	ma sœur,	my *sister*
ton cousin,	thy *cousin, m.*	ta cousine,	thy *cousin, f.*
son père,	his, her *father*	sa mère,	his, her *mother*

l'oncle, *the uncle*	à la maison, *at home*	la plume, *the pen, the feather*
la tante, *the aunt*	le crayon, *the lead pencil*	arrivé, *arrived*
le pain, *the bread*	la main, *the hand*	propre, *clean, fit*
le vin, *the wine*	le train, *the train*	bon, *good*
le jardin, *the garden*	Londres, (silent s) *London*	aussi, *also.*
la maison, *the house*	la Tamise, *the Thames*	

1. *Ton* frère a lu *mon* livre. 2. Il a vu *ton* frère et *ta* sœur. 3. *Ta* sœur a vu *ma* tante. 4. *Ton* pain est bon. 5. *Mon* vin est bon aussi. 6. *Ton* oncle a *une* maison, et *ta* tante a *un* jardin. 7. Votre cousin a bu *mon* vin. 8. Le train est parti. 9. *Ton* crayon est bon. 10. *Ma* main est propre. 11. Londres est sur la Tamise. 12. *Ton* frère a admiré *mon* jardin.

14.

1. Thy cousin has my pencil. 2. He has seen my brother and my sister. 3. My aunt has seen thy pencil and thy pen. 4. Our train has (is) started. 5. Your hand is on the book. 6. My bread is good. 7. My uncle has given the wine to your aunt. 8. My cousin has seen London. 9. Your house is clean, and your garden is magnificent. 10. My brother has found your lead pencil and your pen.

15.

His *brother is ill* } Son frère est malade.
Her *brother is ill*

His *sister is ill* } Sa sœur est malade.
Her *sister is ill*

In French the Possessive Adjectives **mon, ton, son, ma, ta, sa** *agree with the thing possessed, and not with the Possessor as in English.*

l'île, *f. the island*
le nègre, *the negro*
le cœur, *the heart*
la foi, *the faith*
le violon, *the violin*
l'ouvrage, *m. the work*

sincère, *sincere*
sévère, *severe*
appris, *learnt*
dans (s mute) *in*
triste, *sad*
vendu, *sold*.

1. Mon ami a vu *son* père et *sa* mère. 2. Louise a perdu *son* frère et *sa* sœur. 3. Il a perdu *son* crayon et *sa* plume. 4. Elle a aussi perdu *son* crayon et *sa* plume. 5. Mon oncle a vu *sa* sœur et *son* frère. 6. Ma tante a aussi vu *sa* sœur et *son* frère. 7. Il a lu un livre: Robinson Crusoé dans *son* île. 8. *Sa* foi est sincère. 9. *Son* cœur est bon. 10. *Son* maître est sévère. 11. Votre sœur a fini *sa* lecture, elle a aussi fini *son* ouvrage. 12. L'Italien a perdu *son* violon.

16.

1. My cousin has lost his uncle and his aunt. 2. He has sold his house and his garden. 3. His wine is good. 4. Emily is sad, her father is ill. 5. Alfred is sad, his mother is ill. 6. My friend is faithful, his faith is sincere. 7. My sister is faithful, her faith is sincere. 8. Robinson is in his island. 9. My brother has found his pear and his knife. 10. His hand is clean. 11. His reading is easy; her reading is easy.

17.
MUTE FINAL CONSONANTS.

b, d, g, p, s, t, x, z, are generally mute at the end of a word: —

plomb, froid, long, sang, coup, trop, les, nos, Paris, dans, petit, fait, voix, nez, assez.

LIAISON.

The consonant at the end of a word, however, is generally carried on to the following if the latter begins with a vowel or silent h: as,

Vous‿avez (pron. voo‿zahvey). Il est‿arrivé. Un grand‿homme (pron. gran‿tom). Les‿habits. Six‿ans. Son‿ami.

Obs. 1. The t of et is never sounded:— Un père et une mère; but le père est‿arrivé.

Obs. 2. Double consonants are generally pronounced like single consonants (except ss):— arriver, elle, appeler, parrain.

‿ between two words indicates that the final consonant of the first is drawn over and sounded with the second.

La France, *France*	le trésor, *the treasure*	en, dans, *in*
le pays, *the country*	l'Italie, *f. Italy*	assez,* *enough*
l'enfant, *m. & f.* the child	grand, *great, large,* tall, big	long, *long* très, *very*
le canal, *the canal*	petit, *little, small*	utile, *useful*
l'argent, *m. the money,* silver	où, *where,* ou, *or* la gare, *the railway station*	Marie, *Mary.* * *before the noun or adj.*

1. La France est‿un grand pays. 2. Le père est‿arrivé. 3. Où est ton petit‿arbre? 4. Mon‿ami a parlé à ton‿oncle. 5. Florence est‿en Italie. 6. Paul est‿un‿enfant. 7. Marie est‿une enfant. 8. Ton livre est‿assez grand. 9. L'enfant est‿à la maison. 10. Ton‿ami a un petit‿enfant. 11. Le canal est très long. 12. Berlin est‿une ville. 13. L'or est‿un métal très‿utile. 14. Le train est‿arrivé à la gare.

18.

1. Paris is a city. 2. The train has (is) arrived. 3. Where is your little child? 4. My child is in the garden. 5. (The) silver is a metal. 6. The bird is on the little tree. 7. The friend has given the gold to my uncle. 8. Your garden is long enough. 9. A friend is a treasure. 10. (The) iron is very useful. 11. Thy oird is on the tree. 12. My coat is useful.

CONSONANTS.

19.] c *sounds like* k:— *before* a, o, u:— canal, caisse, coq, cour, culture, cuir. *before a consonant (except* h):— clair, croix. *at the end of a word after a vowel:*— lac, bec, duc.

c *sounds like* ss:— *before* e, i, y:— ce, cet, ces, ceci, cymbale, ciel, France, cire, cinq, cent, lance, César. *when it has a cedilla* (ç):— français, ça, leçon, reçu, commençons.

ch *sounds like the English* sh (*not* ch):— chapeau, chaise, chez, cheveu, choc, chute.
qu *sounds like* k (u *not sounded*):— quatre, qui, que, quel, quand.

masc. ce, cet; *fem.* cette, *this, that;*
masc. { ce, *before a consonant:*—
         { cet, *before a vowel or silent* h:—
{ ce roi, *this king*
{ cet ami, *this friend*
{ cet habit, *this coat.*
fem. cette; *as,* cette reine, *this queen;* cette amie, *this friend, f.*
cette habitude, *this habit.*

le ciel, *the heaven,*
  the sky
la leçon, *the lesson*
le prophète, *the prophet*
le (la) domestique, *the servant*
le cadeau, *the present*

le Français, (*subst.*) *the Frenchman*
français (*adj.*) *French*
le concert, *the concert*
reçu, *received*
commencé, *begun*
fait, *made, done*

qui? *who? whom?*
quel? *which? what?*
cela, *that (standing alone)*
c'est, *it is, this is*
oui, *yes*
de, *of, from*
mais, *but.*

1. Le ciel est bleu. 2. Charles a reçu cette lettre. 3. Qui a commencé la leçon? 4. Le maître a commencé la leçon. 5. Qui a fait cela? 6. Mon frère a fait cela. 7. Quel homme a parlé? 8. *Cet* homme a parlé. 9. Qui a donné ma lettre à ton cousin? 10. C'est mon ami qui a donné *cette* lettre à ton cousin et à ta cousine. 11. Qui a frappé *ce* roc? 12. C'est le prophète qui a frappé *ce* roc. 13. Qui a apporté *cette* eau? 14. Il a reçu *ce* crayon, *cet* habit, *cet* argent et *cette* fleur de *cet* enfant.

20.

1. Who has brought this letter? 2. What man has lost this book? 3. This coat is new. 4. This money is for this child. 5. This man has (is) arrived from that town. 6. This lesson is easy. 7. Who has received this present? 8. Which child has begun this lesson? 9. The sky is clear. 10. This Italian has begun the concert.

21.

g *sounds hard before*	g *sounds soft before*
a, o, u :— gant, gond, goutte, gai, Gustave, guerre, aigu; *and* consonants (*except* n):— gloire, gris, grave, anglais.	e, i, y: — genou, germe, affligé, gibier, gymnase, sage, il mangea, nous songeons.

Obs. In gue, gué, gui, (*as*— *guerre, langue, guérir, guise*) *the vowel* u *is not sounded.*

j *sounds like soft* g (*like* s *in leisure*):— jardin, jaloux, jeune, je, projet, joli, jour, jus.

Present Tense of avoir, *to have.*

j'ai, *I have*	ai-je? *have I?*
tu as, *thou hast*	as-tu? *hast thou?*
il (elle) a, *he (she) has*	a-t-il (elle)? *has he (she)?*
on a, *one has*	a-t-on? *has one?*
nous avons, *we have*	avons-nous? *have we?*
vous avez, *you have*	avez-vous? *have you?*
ils (elles) ont, *they have*	ont-ils (elles)? *have they?*

le gant, *the glove*	monsieur, *sir, gentleman*	joué, *m. played*
déjà, *already*	messieurs, *gentlemen, Messrs.*	mangé, *eaten*
le gilet, *the waistcoat*	madame, *my lady, Mrs.*	anglais, *English*
la glace, *the ice*	mesdames, *my ladies*	l'Anglais, *the Englishman*
l'exercice, *f. the exercise*	leur, *their*	affligé, *sad*
le gibier, *the game*	grec, *Greek*	sage, *wise, good (as to*
la guerre, *the war*	mis, *placed, put on*	joli, *pretty. conduct)*

1. *As*-tu mon gant? 2. Oui, j'ai ton gant. 3. Jean *a* un joli jardin. 4. Charles est très affligé. 5. *As*-tu mis ton gilet? 6. Oui, j'ai mis mon gilet. 7. Où *as*-tu joué? 8. J'ai joué dans le jardin. 9. *Avez*-vous déjà mangé votre gâteau? 10. Oui, madame, nous *avons* mangé notre gâteau. 11. *Avez*-vous parlé anglais? 12. Oui, messieurs, nous *avons* parlé anglais. 13. *Ont*-elles parlé français? 14. Oui, mesdames, elles *ont* parlé français.

22.

1. Where hast thou found this glove? 2. Have you seen the palace? 3. The donkey has eaten the grass. 4. Have they sold the game? 5. Did you speak (have you spoken) French? 6. No (sir) but I have spoken Italian. 7. Who has the money? 8. I have the money. 9. Has he learned his lesson? 10. Yes he has already learnt his lesson. 11. Have they seen their brother? 12. Yes, they have seen their brother.

FORMATION OF THE PLURAL.

23.

Singular (*Singulier*).	Plural (*Pluriel*).
le frère, *the brother*	les frères, *the brothers*
la sœur, *the sister*	les sœurs, *the sisters*
l'ami, *m.* ⎫ *the friend*	les⌣amis, *m.* ⎫ *the friends*
l'amie, *f.* ⎭	les⌣amies, *f.* ⎭
ce chien, *this dog*	ces chiens, *these dogs*
cet⌣arbre, *this tree*	ces⌣arbres, *these trees*
cette plume, *this pen*	ces plumes, *these pens.*

General Rule. Substantives *and* **Adjectives** *used in the* **Plural** *number take* **s***; but those which end in* **s, x** *or* **z** *do* **not** *change in the* **Plural.**

la tête, *the head*
le pied, *the foot*
la cerise, *the cherry*
l'orange, *f. the orange*
le bas, *the stocking*
la botte, *the boot*
la noix, *the nut*

le bras, *the arm*
Jean, *John*
la prairie, *the meadow*
la faute, *the fault,*
   mistake
dérangé, *put out of order*
oublié, *forgotten*

sont, *are*
acheté, *bought*
ouvert, *opened, open*
deux, *two*
trois, *three*
quatre, *four*
quand, *when.*

1. Charles et Jean, avez-vous⌣écrit les⌣exercices? 2. Qui a dérangé ces livres? 3. Mon⌣ami Henri a quatre crayons, trois plumes⌣et deux canifs. 4. Ont-elles mangé les cerises? 5. Quand⌣ont⌣ils⌣acheté ces⌣oranges? 6. Avez-vous⌣ouvert les fenêtres? 7. Oui, nous⌣avons⌣ouvert les fenêtres⌣et les portes. 8. Pour qui sont ces cerises? 9. Elles sont pour les⌣enfants et ces pommes sont pour les⌣amies. 10. Ont-ils vu les palais⌣et les jardins? 11. Avez-vous mis les bas? 12. J'ai une tête, deux bras, deux mains⌣et deux pieds.

24.

1. Have they read these books? 2. Has he put on these stockings? 3. Yes, he has put on these stockings and these boots. 4. Have you learnt the lessons? 5. Who has eaten the nuts? 6. Charles has found these flowers in the meadows. 7. You have made three mistakes in these exercises. 8. Where have you bought these trees? 9. You have forgotten the letters and the books. 10. Has she corrected these exercises? 11. Have you admired the palaces and gardens? 12. I have received three nuts from my friend.

FORMATION OF THE PLURAL

25.

Singulier.	Pluriel.
mon frère, *my brother*	mes frères, *my brothers*
ma sœur, *my sister*	mes sœurs, *my sisters*
ton cousin, *m.* ⎫ *thy cousin*	tes cousins, *m.* ⎫ *thy cousins*
ta cousine, *f.* ⎭	tes cousines, *f.* ⎭
son ami, *his (her) friend*	ses amis, *his (her) friends*
sa plume, *his (her) pen*	ses plumes, *his (her) pens*
notre canif, *our penknife*	nos canifs, *our penknives*
votre maître, *your master*	vos maîtres, *your masters*
leur fils, *their son*	leurs fils, *their sons*

la musique, *the music*
le libraire, *the bookseller*
la librairie, *the bookseller's shop or business*
le parapluie, *the umbrella*
le bagage, *the luggage*
la cloche, *the bell*
le voyageur, *the traveller*
amené, *led, brought*

le voisin, *m.* ⎫ *the neighbour*
la voisine, *f.* ⎭
manqué, *missed, failed*
attendu, *waited, expected*
entendu, *heard, learned, understood*
longtemps, *a long time*
ici, *here*   là, *there*
chez, { *at the house (shop) of,*
{ *at the . . . . 's.*

1. Où as-tu acheté *ton* papier, *ta* plume et *tes* crayons? 2. J'ai acheté *mes* canifs, *ma* plume et *mes* crayons chez le libraire. 3. Quand a-t-il reçu *mon* livre, *ma* lettre et *mes* papiers? 4. Ont-ils fini *leurs* exercices? 5. Ont-elles commencé *leurs* lectures? 6. *Vos* cousins ont apporté *leurs* violons et *vos* cousins ont amené *leurs* amies. 7. Les voyageurs ont perdu *leur* bagage. 8. *Mes* sœurs ont trouvé *leurs* parapluies. 9. *Nos* voisins et *nos* voisines ont fermé *leurs* maisons. 10. *Tes* amis sont aussi *mes* amis. 11. *Votre* tante et *vos* cousins ont manqué le train. 12. *Notre* oncle et *nos* cousines ont attendu longtemps.

26.

1. My uncle, my aunt and my cousins have brought their friends. 2. His friends (f.) are here. 3. Have you eaten your cake and your apples? 4. We have eaten our cake and our apples. 5. Have they brought their gloves? 6. Yes, they have brought their gloves and their umbrellas. 7. My friends have brought their books. 8. Our neighbours have brought their friends. 9. Where are your umbrellas and your gloves? 10. Have they found their luggage? 11. These travellers have missed the train. 12. Have they heard the bell?

27.

s *sounds like* ss *at the beginning of a word; in the middle after consonants only:* — sage, le sel, siffler, le sol, absolu, observe, constant.

s *sounds like* z, (1) *between two vowels:* — la maison, saisir, le cousin. (2) *in liaisons (see 17):* — les‿amis, mes‿habits, ces‿hommes.

z (*initial*) *sounds as in English:* — le zéro, le zèle, la zône.

Present of **être**, *to be*.

je suis, *I am*
tu es, *thou art*
il (elle) est, *he (she) is*
on est, *one is*
nous sommes, *we are*
vous êtes, *you are*
ils (elles) sont, *they are.*

suis-je? *am I?*
es-tu? *art thou?*
est-il (elle)? *is he (she)?*
est-on? *is one?*
sommes-nous? *are we?*
êtes-vous? *are you?*
sont-ils (elles)? *are they?*

Practice:— 1 am at school, thou art at church, etc. Am I young? Art thou tired? etc.

le soir, *the evening*
le devoir, *the duty, task*
le zèle, *the zeal*
à l'école, *f. at school*
à l'église, *f. at church*
riche, *rich*

parce que, *because*
jeune, *young*
fatigué, *tired*
cher (*fem.* chère) *dear, expensive*
content, *contented, satisfied*
la table, *the table.*

1. *Es*-tu mon ami? 2. Oui, mon cher Gustave, je *suis* ton ami. 3. *Est*-il arrivé? 4. Oui, il *est* arrivé ce soir. 5. Mon cousin *est* aussi arrivé. 6. *Êtes*-vous content? 7. *Êtes*-vous sage? 8. Je *suis* content parce que je *suis* sage. 9. *Est*-il riche? 10. Non, mais il *est* content. 11. *Est*-elle jeune? 12. *Sont*-elles à l'église? 13. Non, elles *sont* à l'école. 14. *Est*-il à la maison? 15. Oui, il *est* à la maison.

28.

1. I am young. 2. Thou art tired. 3. He is satisfied. 4. She is rich. 5. One is contented. 6. Your are at home. 7. They are at church. 8. Is he in Paris? 9. Are you my friend? 10. Is she your friend? 11. Are they your cousins? 12. Are they (*f.*) your cousins. 13. Are they at home? 14. Are they from London. 15. Is she at school?

29.

Masculine.		Feminine.	Masculine.		Feminine.
grand,	*great*	grande,	français,	*French*	française,
petit,	*little*	petite.	fatigué,	*tired*	fatiguée.

General Rule. *The* **Feminine of Adjectives** (*and Substantives*) *is formed by adding* **e** *mute to the masculine termination; but Adjectives which end in* **e** *mute in the* **Masculine** *remain unchanged in the* **Feminine Singular:** *as,*

Masculine.		Feminine.	Masculine.		Feminine.
utile,	*useful*	utile,	difficile,	*difficult*	difficile,
timide,	*timid*	timide.	riche,	*rich*	riche.

An Adjective agrees in Gender *and* Number *with the Substantive or Pronoun to which it relates; that is—*

(1) *An Adjective takes the Sign of the* Feminine *when the Substantive or Pronoun which it qualifies is in the* Feminine: *as,*

Masc. Ton petit cousin est fatigué.   Fem. Ta petite cousine est fatiguée.

(2) *An Adjective takes the Sign of the* Plural (*generally* **s**, *see 23*) *when the Substantive or Pronoun is used in the* Plural: *as,*

Sing. Le bon chien est utile.   Plur. Le bons chiens sont utiles.

Obs. *If the* **Feminine** *Substantive is in the* **Plural,** *the Adjective takes the Sign of both* **Feminine** *and* **Plural:—**

Masculine Singular.	**Feminine Plural.**
Ton petit cousin est fatigué.	Tes petites cousines sont fatiguées.
difficile, *difficult*	amusant, *amusing, entertaining*
fort, *strong*	le thème, *the exercise*
écrit, *written*	si, *so.*

1. Les *bons* livres sont *utiles.* 2. Mon cousin est *grand.* 3. Ma cousine est *grande.* 4. Es-tu *malade?* 5. Êtes-vous *malades?* 6. Le voyageur est *fatigué.* 7. Les voyageurs sont *fatigués.* 8. Mon livre *anglais* est *amusant.* 9. Ta lettre *anglaise* est *amusante.* 10. Tes livres *anglais* sont *amusants.* 11. Tes lettres *anglaises* sont *amusantes.* 12. Sont-elles *riches?* 13. Non, mais elles sont *contentes.*

30.

1. (The) good dogs are faithful. 2. My cousins are young. 3. Your neighbours are rich. 4. We are your faithful[a] friends.[1] 5. Have you written your exercises? 6. Are they difficult? 7. No, they are easy. 8. My dear friends, are you tired? 9. Yes, we are very tired. 10. Your French[2] books[1] are very amusing. 11. These readings are useful. 12. My little friends are timid.

31.

h *is silent in most words derived from Latin:* —
l'homme, l'histoire, l'herbe, habile, l'habitude.

h *is* **aspirate** *in most words not derived from Latin:* —
la 'haine, le 'hasard, la 'honte, la 'harpe, la 'hâte, 'haut.

Obs. th *is* never *pronounced as in English;* t *alone is sounded:* — le thé (pron. *tay*) *the tea.*

Remember that

before a word beginning with a **silent** h *(as before a vowel)*	*before a word beginning with an* **aspirate** h *(as bef. other cons.)*
(1) le, la, *the, drop their vowel* (l'): — l'homme, l'habitude.	(1) le, la *never drop their vowel:* — le 'hasard, la 'honte.
(2) ce, *(m.) this, takes a* t (cet): — cet homme, cet habit.	(2) ce, *(masc.) never takes a* t: — ce 'hasard, ce 'hareng.
(3) *the final consonant of the preceding word is drawn over (liaison, see Expl. 8):* — les grands‿hommes, mes‿habits.	(3) *the final consonant of the preceding word is never drawn over:* — les grands 'hasards, les 'harpes.

l'histoire, *f. the history, story*
l'hiver, *m. the winter*
le 'héros, *the hero*
la 'hauteur, *the height*
la 'haie, *the hedge*
la 'harpe, *the harp*
la 'Hollande, *Holland*
le 'hameçon, *the fishhook*
froid, *cold*
la colline, *the hill*
'hardi, *bold*
vert, *green*
'haut, *high*
considérable, *considerable*
combattu, *fought*
raconté, *related*
devant, *before (as to place)*
avant, *before (as to time and order).*

1. L'hiver est froid. 2. Cet hiver mon cousin a été à Paris. 3. As-tu mis ton habit neuf? 4. Où as-tu acheté ton hameçon? 5. Le héros a combattu pour sa patrie. 6. Qui a raconté ces histoires? 7. Cet arbre est haut. 8. Ce héros est hardi. 9. La haie devant la maison est très haute. 10. La hauteur de cette colline est considérable.

32.

1. I have read the history of this hero. 2. Have you read the history of (the) Holland? 3. I have lost my book. 4. They are on the high hill. 5. This hedge is green. 6. This harp is splendid. 7. This coat is new. 8. This grass is very high. 9. This man has been in (en) Holland. 10. This hero is honoured in his country.

VERB ÊTRE.

33.
Present of être, *to be*, negatively and interrogatively.

je ne suis pas, *I am not,*	ne suis-je pas, *am I not?* etc.
tu n'es pas, *etc.*	n'es-tu pas,
il (elle) n'est pas,	n'est-il (elle) pas,
on n'est pas,	n'est-on pas,
nous ne sommes pas,	ne sommes-nous pas,
vous n'êtes pas,	n'êtes-vous pas,
ils (elles) ne sont pas,	ne sont-ils (elles) pas?

Read and translate all sentences in Ex. 28 negatively.

la lettre, *the letter*
heureux, *happy*
malheureux, *unhappy*
appliqué, *diligent*
pourquoi, *why*
toujours, *always.*

Obs. The following Past Participles of Verbs (most of which express going or coming), are conjugated in French with the Auxiliary Verb être, *to be:*—

allé, *gone*
arrivé, *arrived*
entré, *entered, come in*
retourné, *returned, gone back*
tombé, *fallen*
resté, *stayed, remained*
parti, *departed, set out, left*
sorti, *gone out*
venu, *come*
revenu, *come back.*

1. *N'es-tu pas* mon ami, Charles? 2. Oui, mon cher Gustave, je suis ton ami. 3. *N'êtes-vous pas* notre voisin? 4. Non, monsieur, je *ne* suis *pas* votre voisin. 5. *Ne* sommes-nous *pas* heureux quand nous avons fait nos devoirs? 6. Oui, nous sommes toujours heureux, quand nous avons fait nos devoirs. 7. Qui est le maître de cette école? 8. C'est monsieur Albert qui est le maître de cette école. 9. Sont-elles à la maison? 10. Non, madame, elles *ne* sont *pas* à la maison. 11. Pourquoi êtes-vous si tristes, mes chers amis? 12. Nous *ne* sommes *pas* tristes.

34.

1. Are they not your neighbours (m. & f.)? 2. No, they are not our neighbours, but they are our friends (m. & f.). 3. Are you the master of this school? 4. No, I am not the master of this school. 5. Is she not at home? 6. Why are you not diligent, my children? 7. We are diligent. 8. Are they not your friends? 9. No, they are not our friends, but they are our neighbours. 10. Is he not satisfied? 11. No, he is not satisfied. 12. Are they not very bold? 13. Are they not unhappy? 14. No, they are not unhappy, they are happy.

VERB AVOIR. 17

35.
Present of Avoir, *to have.*
negatively *and* interrogatively.

je n'ai pas, *I have not, etc.*
tu n'as pas,
il (elle) n'a pas,
on n'a pas,
nous n'avons pas,
vous n'avez pas,
ils (elles) n'ont pas;

n'ai-je pas, *have I not? etc.*
n'as-tu pas,
n'a-t-il (-elle) pas,
n'a-t-on pas,
n'avons-nous pas,
n'avez-vous pas,
n'ont-ils (-elles) pas?

Read and translate all the sentences of Ex. 22 **negatively.**

le temps, *the time, the weather*
dîné, *dined*
déjeuné, *breakfasted*
pas encore, *not yet*

pas même, *not even*
aujourd'hui, *to-day*
le cheval, *the horse*
bon, *m.* } *good*
bonne, *f.*

la servante, *the maidservant*
la chambre, *the room*
la saison, *the season*
comment? *how?* what!
mais, *but.*

1. As-tu déjà dîné? 2. Non je *n'ai pas* encore dîné, je *n'ai pas* même déjeuné. 3. Comment, tu *n'as pas* encore déjeuné? 4. Je *n'ai pas* eu le temps. 5. *N'*a-t-il *pas* assez mangé? 6. Non, il *n'a pas* encore assez mangé. 7. Nous *n'*avons *pas* encore appris nos leçons aujourd'hui. 8. Avez-vous un beau jardin? 9. Non, monsieur, mais nous avons une prairie. 10. A-t-il un domestique? 11. Non, il a une servante. 12. Ont-ils un tableau dans la chambre? 13. Oui, ils ont un tableau superbe dans la chambre.

36.

1. Have I not your letter? 2. Hast thou not a good horse? 3. Has he not a large house? 4. Has she not a pretty child? 5. Have we not a good season? 6. Have you not two dogs? 7. Have they not a useful[2] book[1]? 8. Has he not a lesson to-day? 9. Has she not yet breakfasted? 10. Have you received a letter? 11. Has he not three books? 12. Has she a friend?

Answer the above questions in French, both **affirmatively** *and* **negatively.**

37.

Le temps est-il beau?	*Is the weather fine?*
Votre santé est-elle bonne?	*Is your health good?*
Les arbres sont-ils hauts?	*Are the trees high?*
Les étoiles sont-elles nombreuses?	*Are the stars numerous?*
Ton frère a-t-il un cheval?	*Has thy brother a horse?*
Tes sœurs ont-elles une leçon?	*Have thy sisters a lesson?*

la santé, *the health*
l'encre, *f. the ink*
la ville, *the town*
en ville, *in town (out*
l'écolier, *m.* } *the scholar, the pupil*
l'écolière, *f.*

l'artiste, *m. & f. the artist*
aimable, *amiable*
chaud, *warm*
voyagé, *travelled*
le village, *the village.*

1. Est-il fort? 2. Ton *frère* est-*il* fort? 3. Ta *sœur* est-*elle* forte? 4. Tes *amis* sont-*ils* aimables? 5. Tes *amies* sont-*elles* aimables? 6. A-t-il voyagé? 7. Ton *ami* a-t-il voyagé? 8. Ta *cousine* a-t-*elle* voyagé? 9. Vos *voisins* ont-*ils* voyagé? 10. Leurs *voisines* ont-*elles* voyagé? 11. Notre *frère* n'est-*il* pas venu? 12. Votre *tante* n'est-*elle* pas partie? 13. Ces *écoliers* ne sont-*ils* pas appliqués? 14. Leurs *fleurs* ne sont-*elles* pas jolies? 15. Votre *santé* est-*elle* bonne, madame? 16. Merci, mon enfant, elle est bonne.

In the following sentences supply an appropriate **Substantive** *for Subject, and give an answer in full, both* **affirmative** *and* **negative**:—

17. Est-il (elle) à la maison? 18. Sont-ils (elles) à l'école? 19. N'est-il (elle) pas à l'église? 20. Ne sont-ils (elles) pas en ville? 21. A-t-il (m. & f. sing. & plur.) fait son (leur) devoir? 22. N'a-t-il (m. & f. sing. & plur.) pas voyagé en Hollande?

38.

1. Is their health good? 2. Is not this ink very pale? 3. Are the doors and windows not open? 4. No, they are not open. 5. Have the travellers lost their luggage? 6. Is not the summer warm? 7. Is the winter not cold? 8. Is this artist rich or poor? 9. Has not the scholar done his duty? 10. Has (is) your brother arrived? 11. Have your friends travelled? 12. Has the scholar a lesson?

ADJECTIVES.

39.

Adjectives ending in **f** *in the* Masculine *change this* **f** *into* ve *in the* Feminine; *those ending in* **x** *change this* **x** *into* se *in the* Feminine; *as,—*

actif, active, *active,* actif, actives.
heureux, heureuse, *happy,* heureux, heureuses.

(See "Eugène's Comparative French Grammar", § 33).

Adjectives denoting names of nations *and* colours *stand after the Substantive:—*

la langue française, *the 'French' language,*
un habit noir, *a 'black' coat.*

Form the feminine of the following Adjectives:— laborieux, simple, neuf, glorieux, modeste, court, avide, attentif, fameux, mauvais, vif, africain, asiatique, victorieux.

le prince, *the prince*   le guerrier, *the warrior*   latin, *latin*
le pardon, *the pardon*   allemand, *German*   vertueux, *virtuous*
la version, *the translation* mauvais, *bad*   laborieux, *industrious*
la Russie, *Russia*   délicieux, *delicious*   voici, *here is*
vénéneux, *poisonous*   populeux, *populous*   voilà, *there is*
le cordonnier,*the shoemaker* studieux, *studious*   la grammaire,*the grammar.*

1. Ce jeune homme est-il *actif* et *laborieux?* 2. Non, il n'est pas *actif*, mais sa sœur est très *active* et *laborieuse.* 3. Où avez-vous acheté cette grammaire *allemande?* 4. J'ai acheté cette grammaire *allemande* chez ce libraire. 5. Ces pommes ne sont-elles pas *mauvaises?* 6. Non, elles sont *délicieuses.* 7. Où avez-vous trouvé cette fleur *bleue?* 8. Nous avons trouvé ces fleurs *bleues* dans votre *petit* jardin. 9. Quand avez-vous écrit ces lettres *françaises?* 10. Le cordonnier a-t-il apporté mes bottes *neuves?* 11. Vos versions *latines* sont-elles *faciles?* 12. Les villes *anglaises* sont-elles *populeuses?* 13. Vos histoires *anglaises* sont-elles *amusantes?* 14. La Russie est-elle un *grand* pays?

40.

1. Are you happy, Louisa? 2. No, I am not happy. 3. Why are you unhappy? 4. We have lost our sister. 5. Why is your cousin (m. & f.) not active? 6. Pardon [me], he (she) is very active. 7. The Black[2] Prince[1] was a courageous warrior. 8. Is your young cousin (f.) studious? 9. Are their boots new? 10. Are your neighbours (m. & f.) virtuous? 11. There is an unhappy child. 12. Is this plant poisonous?

ADJECTIVES.

41.

cruel, cruelle, *cruel*
pareil, pareille, *like, such*
quel? quelle? *which? what?*
italien, italienne, *Italian*
bon, bonne, *good*
bas, basse, *low.*

Adjectives ending in el, eil, en, on *and most adjectives in* s *double their final consonant and add* e *in the feminine.*

In like manner **Substantives** *may be made feminine:—*

le juif, *the Jew*
la juive, *the Jewess*
le lion, *the lion*
la lionne, *the lioness.*

Adjectives ending in er, et, *take a grave accent:—*
cher, chère; complet, complète.

la langue, *the tongue, the language*
la religion, *the religion*
la montre, *the watch*
la maladie { *the illness* / *the disease*
l'avarice, *f. the avarice*
la passion, *the passion*
la connaissance, { *the knowledge* / *the acquaintance*
chrétien, *christian*
consolant, *consoling*
las, *tired*
honteux, *disgraceful*
ancien, *ancient, old*
intéressant, *interesting*
étudié, *studied, learned*
Henriette, *Henrietta*
la conduite, *the behaviour.*

1. Avez-vous étudié la langue *italienne?* 2. Non, monsieur, mais j'ai étudié la langue *française* et la langue *latine.* 3. Cette eau est très *bonne.* 4. La religion *chrétienne* est *consolante.* 5. *Quelle* montre avez-vous là? 6. C'est une montre *anglaise.* 7. Est-elle *neuve?* 8. Non, elle n'est pas *neuve*, mais elle est encore *bonne.* 9. Mes sœurs ne sont pas encore *lasses.* 10. La lionne est *cruelle.* 11. *Quelle* maladie a-t-il? 12. *Quel* homme a amené ce cheval? 13. L'avarice est une passion *honteuse.* 14. Les montres *anglaises* sont très *bonnes.*

42.

1. (The) ancient history in interesting. 2. Is your aunt tired? 3. I have seen a lion and a lioness. 4. Such[a] (a)[1] behaviour is disgraceful. 5. The Italian language is very easy. 6. Are you tired, Henrietta? 7. These houses are very low. 8. Which book have you lost? 9. The water is low. 10. What lesson have you for this evening? 11. The knowledge of the French language is very useful. 12. You are not happy, my cousins (f.), because you are not industrious.

43.
de, of, from; à, *to, at, in.*

de Londres, *of (from) London;* à Londres, *to (at, in) London*
de Bruxelles, *of (from) Brussels;* à Bruxelles, *to (at, in) Brussels*
d'Athènes, *of (from) Athens;* à Athènes, *to (at, in) Athens.*

d' *stands instead of* de *before words beginning with a vowel or silent* h.

The English in, (at) *is rendered in French by* à, en *or* dans:—

(1) *by* à *before names of* towns *or* places:—
à Paris, à la maison, à l'église;

(2) *by* en *before names of* countries *without article:*—
en France, en Amérique;

(3) *by* dans *before names of* countries & places *with the Article:*—
dans la France méridionale, dans l'Amérique du Nord.

la rue, *the street*	Douvres, *Dover*	irlandais, *Irish*
le peintre, *the painter*	Venise, *Venice*	à présent, *at present,*
l'étudiant, *m. the student*	Vienne, *Vienna*	*now*
Genève, *Geneva*	Moscou, *Moscow*	le négociant, *the merchant*
la Suisse, *Switzerland*	l'Angleterre, *f. England*	le marchand, *the trades-*
Gênes, *Genoa*	d'où? *whence, where from?*	*man*

1. D'où est votre maître? 2. Notre maître est *de* Bordeaux. 3. Où est votre servante irlandaise? 4. Elle est à présent *à* Dublin. 5. Votre ami est-il allé *à* Gênes? Non, il n'est pas allé *à* Vienne, mais il est allé *à* Venise. 6. Où sont vos jeunes sœurs? 7. Elles sont encore *à* Genève. 8. Où est Genève? 9. Genève est *en* Suisse. 10. Monsieur Albert est-il *de* Rome? 11. Non, il est *d'*Athènes. 12. Ce peintre est revenu *d'*Italie. 13. Les rues *de* Londres sont-elles grandes? 14. Les maisons *de* Paris sont-elles hautes? 15. Avez-vous été *en* Angleterre? 16. Oui, j'ai été *à* Londres.

44.

1. Where is this student from? 2. This student is from Dover. 3. Where is he now? 4. He is now at Caen. 5. Have (are) the travellers not come* from Berlin? 6. No, they have come* from Moscow. 7. Where is Moscow? 8. Moscow is in Russia. 9. Has** your master returned from Paris? 10. No, he is now at Rome. 11. Have (are) the merchants arrived* in England? 12. Yes, they are now in London. 13. Where have (are) these young painters come* from? 14. They have come* from Italy. 15. From Genoa or from Rome? 16. No, they have come* from Florence.

*plural. **Ex. 33. Obs.

45.

| Avoir, | PAST INDEFINITE. | Être, |

Past Part.:— eu, *had;*   été, *been.*

j'ai eu, *I have had, etc.*	j'ai été, *I have been, etc.*
tu as eu	tu as été
il (elle, on) a eu	il (elle, on) a été
nous avons eu	nous avons été
vous avez eu	vous avez été
ils (elles) ont eu.	ils (elles) ont été.
Je n'ai pas eu, *I have not had, etc.*	Je n'ai pas été, *I have not been, etc.*
Ai-je eu? *Have I had? etc.*	Ai-je été? *Have I been? etc.*
N'ai-je pas eu? *Have I not had?*	N'ai-je pas été? *Have I not been?*

    For *practice form sentences by adding appropriate Substantives to the Verbs in the first column, and Adjectives or names of places to those in the second: as,*

J'ai eu un ami, etc.	J'ai été malade, etc.
Ai-je eu une leçon? etc.	Ai-je été récompensé? etc.
Je n'ai pas eu le livre, etc.	Je n'ai pas été à Bordeaux, etc.
N'ai-je pas eu votre encrier? etc.	N'ai-je pas été à Paris? etc.

le prix, *the prize, the price*	Vienne, *Vienna*	récompensé, *rewarded*
Édimbourg, *Edinburgh*	le déjeuner, *breakfast*	hier, *yesterday*
l'officier, *m. the officer*	le médecin, *the physician*	le dernier, *the last*
l'an, *m.* l'année, *f. the year*	la médecine, *the medecine*	l'encrier, *m. the inkstand*
la semaine, *the week*	puni, *punished*	le matin, *the morning.*

    1. *As-tu* déjà *eu* ta leçon, mon jeune ami? 2. Oui, monsieur, *j'ai eu* ma leçon ce matin. 3. Votre maître *a-t-il été* ici? 4. Non, madame, *il n'a pas été* ici. 5. Qui *a eu* le prix? 6. Mon ami Henri *a eu* le prix. 7. Quand *avez-vous été* à Édimbourg? 8. *Nous avons été* hier à Édimbourg. 9. Les officiers *ont-ils été* à Châlons? 10. Non, les officiers *ont été* à Versailles. 11. Pourquoi *avez-vous été* puni? 12. *J'ai été* puni parce que *je n'ai pas été* sage.

46.

    1. Have you already been in London, Sir? 2. Yes, Sir, I have been in London this week. 3. Has he had a lesson with his brother? 4. Yes, he has had two lessons. 5. Have you not been in Venice this summer? 6. No, I have been in Vienna. 7. Have they not been punished? 8. No, Sir, they have been rewarded. 9. Has the physician been here? 10. Yes, he has been here this morning. 11. Have the children been at school? 12. No, they have been to church.

47.

Subject (*Nom.*)
Direct Object (*Acc.*) } Guillaume, *William*
Indirect Object { (*Gen.*) de Guillaume, *of (from) William, William's*
{ (*Dat.*) à Guillaume, *to William.*

Nom. & Acc. Alfred, *Alfred*   un ami, *a friend*
Gen. d'Alfred, *of (from) Alfred,*   d'un ami, *of (from) a friend,*
        Alfred's   *a friend's*
Dat. à Alfred, *to Alfred*   à un ami, *to a friend.*

Decline thus: — Émilie, Charles, une fleur, ce couteau, etc.

Observe that the English Possessive case can be rendered in French in one way only — that is by putting the preposition **de** before the possessor: as,

The books of my friend } Les livres de mon ami.
My friend's books

I received this book from my friend = J'ai reçu ce livre de mon ami.

Practice:— a father's love, the king's palace, my friend's gloves; Byron's poem's, your cousin's house; their mother's death; your child's hat.

l'amour, *m. the love, af-*   la tâche, *the task*   la clef, (*f.* silent) *the key*
  fection   la tache, *the spot, stain*   le poëme, *the poem*
l'œuvre, *f. the work*   avec, *with*   le martyr, *the martyr*
la mort, *the death*   François, *Francis*   de qui, *of (from) whom*
le cahier, *the copybook*   la règle, *f. the rule*

1. As-tu reçu ce cadeau *de* ta cousine? 2. As-tu donné ton livre *à* Charles? 3. Non, j'ai donné mon livre *à* François. 4. A-t-il prêté son cahier *à* Émile? 5. Avez-vous écrit *à* votre frère? 6. La tâche *de* Louise est-elle difficile? 7. Qui êtes-vous, monsieur? 8. Je suis le cousin *de* votre ami. 9. Êtes-vous le médecin *de* ma tante? 10. Avez-vous appris les règles *de* votre grammaire? 11. *De* qui as-tu reçu cette belle montre? 12. *A* qui as-tu montré la clef? 13. Le livre *d'*Alice est-il amusant? 14. Les lettres *de* votre tante sont-elles intéressantes?

48.

1. Have you read Byron's poems? 2. No, I have not read Byron's poems, but I have read Fox's Martyrs. 3. Is Henry's Latin book easy? 4. Has* your father's friend come? 5. Yes, he has come with our physician's son. 6. Have you written to your master? 7. No, Sir, but I have written to our bookseller. 8. Has your brother's lesson been easy? 9. Has your friend seen our neighbour's garden? 10. William's sister has not written to our cousin. 11. Our gardener's son has not yet come. 12. From whom have you received these letters?   *Ex. 33. Obs.

49.

de le = du,   of (from) the   de les = des,
à le = au,   to (at) the   à les = aux.

When de or à stand before le or les, they are contracted into one word, as above. (See Eugène's French Grammar, Introd. § 31.)

But de and à are never contracted with either la or l'.

Nom. } le frère, *the brother*   les frères, *the brothers*
Acc.
Gen. du frère, { *of (from) the brother* / *the brother's*   des frères, *of (from) the brothers*
Dat. au frère, *to the brother*   aux frères, *to the brothers*

l'ami, *the friend*   les amis, *the friends*
de l'ami, { *of (from) the friend* / *the friend's*   des amis, *of (from) the friends*
à l'ami, *to the friend*   aux amis, *to the friends*

l'homme, *the man*   les hommes, *the men*
de l'homme, { *of (from) the man* / *the man's*   des hommes, *of (from) the men*
à l'homme, *to the man*   aux hommes, *to the men*

la sœur, *the sister*   les sœurs, *the sisters*
de la sœur, { *of (from) the sister* / *the sister's*   des sœurs, *of (from) the sisters*
à la sœur, *to the sister*   aux sœurs, *to the sisters*

l'eau, *the water*   les eaux, *the waters*
de l'eau, { *of (from) the water* / *the water's*   des eaux, *of (from) the waters*
à l'eau, *to the water*   aux eaux, *to the waters*.

Dieu, *God*
le monde, *the world*
le goût, *the taste*
la bière, *the beer*
le fruit, *the fruit*
le nom, *the name*
la princesse, *the princess*
le colonel, *the colonel*
le capitaine, *the captain*
l'institutrice, *the governess*
la bonne, *the nursery maid, servant*
le commerce, *the commerce*

le teint, *the complexion*
la rive, *the bank, shore*
le conseil, *the advice, counsel*
le chasseur, *the hunter*
la trace, *the trace, track*
le lièvre, *the hare*
la vie, *the life*
la capitale, *the capital*
le Portugal, *Portugal*
la France, *France*
l'empereur, *the emperor*
la faim, *the hunger*

le soldat, *the soldier*
la paix, *the peace*
le Prussien, *the Prussian*
l'ennemi, masc. *the enemy*
la tour, *the tower*
le tour, *the turn, round*
suivi, *followed*
Lisbonne, *Lisbon*
observé, *observed*
exposé, *exposed*
joint, *joined*
mûr, *ripe*.

DECLENSION.

1. Avez-vous apporté les livres *du* frère, *de l'*oncle et *de la* tante? 2. Dieu est le maître *du* monde et le roi *des* rois. 3. Le maître a parlé *de la* leçon *de l'*écolier. 4. Le goût *du* vin et *de la* bière est agréable. 5. Les fruits *des* arbres *du* jardin sont mûrs. 6. Édouard est le nom *du* prince et Henriette est le nom *de la* princesse. 7. A-t-il observé les règles *de la* grammaire? 8. Louis Philippe a été le roi *des* Français. 9. Nous avons parlé *des* amis *du* colonel. 10. Avez-vous écrit *au* frère *du* capitaine? 11. Non, monsieur, nous avons écrit une lettre *à la* sœur *de l'*institutrice, et deux lettres *à l'*amie *de la* bonne. 12. Ont-ils montré leurs thèmes *aux* maîtres *du* collége? 13. N'avez-vous pas admiré le teint *des* Anglaises? 14. Les rives *du* Rhône et *de la* Seine sont charmantes. 15. Avez-vous suivi les conseils *du* médecin? 16. Les chiens *des* chasseurs ont suivi les traces *des* lièvres.

50.

1. Has she not admired the palaces of the king and of the queen? 2. The life of man is short. 3. Paris is the capital of (the) France, and Lisbon is the capital of (the) Portugal. 4. The merchant has spoken of (the) commerce, and the soldier of (the) war and (of the) peace. 5. I have not found the physician's son at home. 6. The poor [man] is exposed to (the) hunger and (to the) cold. 7. The Prussians are the enemies of the French. 8. The tower of the church of the village is very high. 9. The soldiers of the Emperor of the French have joined the soldiers of the Queen of England. 10. Francis is my brother's name. 11. Is your friend's health good? 12. The emperor's soldiers have joined the enemy.

51.

combien de, { *how much* / *how many*}
il y a, *there is, there are*
y a-t-il? *is there? are there?*
font*, *make, are*
fois, *time (in multiplicat.)*
le printemps, *the spring*
l'été, *m. the summer*

l'automne, (*m* mute) *m.* *the autumn*
l'hiver, *m. the winter*
le jour, *the day*
le mois, *the month*
la classe, *the class*
le doigt,† *the finger*
la chaise, *the chair*

dimanche, *Sunday*
lundi, *Monday*
mardi, *Tuesday*
mercredi, *Wednesday*
jeudi, *Thursday*
vendredi, *Friday*
samedi, *Saturday*
le pont, *the bridge.*

*3d p. plur. Indicat. Present of faire. †*gt* mute. The days of the week are Masc.

NUMERALS.

1, un, une, *f.*	8, huit	15, quinze
2, deux	9, neuf	16, seize
3, trois	10, dix	17, dix-sept
4, quatre	11, onze	18, dix-huit
5, cinq	12, douze	19, dix-neuf
6, six	13, treize	20, vingt
7, sept	14, quatorze	21, vingt et un.

The final consonants of cinq, six, sept, huit, neuf, dix, *are pronounced* (1) *when these numbers are standing alone:—*
il y en a cinq, six, sept, huit, neuf, dix.

(2) *before a* **vowel** *or* **silent h** (*see Lesson 17*):—
cinq arbres, sept heures.

The final consonant is **not** *pronounced before a Substantive or Adjective beginning with a consonant:—* cinq maisons, sept harpes.

Pronounce the following numbers in French:— 10, 14, 9, 2, 13, 8, 19, 11, 20, 15, 1, 14, 3, 17, 5, 12, 6, 16, 7, 4.

1. L'année a *quatre* saisons: le printemps, l'été, l'automne et l'hiver. 2. Combien de maisons y a-t-il dans cette rue? 3. Il y a *vingt* maisons. 4. Combien de jours y a-t-il dans une semaine? 5. Combien font *quatre* et *douze; cinq* et *neuf; huit* et *onze; treize* et *cinq; trois* et *seize?* 6. Nous sommes *douze* dans notre classe. 7. Combien font *quatre* fois *cinq? trois* fois *six? deux* fois *huit?* 8. Combien de doigts as-tu? 9. Combien de fautes y a-t-il dans votre thème? 10. La semaine a *sept* jours: dimanche, lundi, mardi, mercredi, jeudi, vendredi et samedi.

52.

1. This town has three churches, twenty streets and four gates. 2. The year has twelve months, the month has four weeks, the week has seven days. 3. How many are 9 and 8, 7 and 13, 8 and 11; 4 times 4, 3 times 5, 3 times 6? 4. We are eighteen in our class. 5. There are five bridges and four gates in this town. 6. How many rooms are there in this house? 7. There are twelve rooms. 8. In this room there are three tables and eight chairs. 9. There are twenty of them (they are twenty) in the French class. 10. I have two hands and ten fingers.

53.

Imperfect (*Imparfait*) of **Avoir**, *to have:* —

1. j'avais, *I had*	Avais-je? *had I?* etc.
tu avais, *thou hadst*	avais-tu? etc.
il (elle) avait, *he (she) had*	Je n'avais pas, *I had not*, etc.
nous avions, *we had*	tu n'avais pas, etc.
vous aviez, *you had*	N'avais-je pas? *had I not?* etc.
ils (elles) avaient *they had.*	n'avais-tu pas? etc.
Il y avait, *there was (were)*	Y avait-il? *was (were) there?*
Il n'y avait pas, *there was (were) not,*	N'y avait-il pas? *was (were) there not?*

la bonté, *the kindness*	la forêt, *the forest, wood*	cherché, *looked for, sought*
le dessin, *the drawing*	la rame*, *the oar*	pris, *taken*
le dessein, *the design*	la poésie, *the poetry*	par, *by*
le verre, *the glass*	maintenant, *now*	avoir raison, *to be right*
le Romain, *the Roman*	autrefois, *formerly*	avoir tort, *to be wrong*
l'armée, *f. the army*	apprendre, *to learn*	

*la rame de papier, *the ream of paper.*

For practice put the verb **avoir** *in all sentences of Ex. 21 in the Imperfect Tense.*

1. L'an dernier nous *avions* la guerre; maintenant nous avons la paix. 2. *N'aviez*-vous *pas* pris une leçon de dessin? 3. Mon oncle *avait* autrefois une grande maison. 4. *N'avait*-elle *pas* une leçon à apprendre? 5. *Avaient*-ils raison ou tort? 6. Mon voisin *avait* raison, mais mon cousin *avait* tort. 7. *Avais*-tu appris tes leçons? 8. Non, je n'*avais* pas appris mes leçons. 9. Il *avait* un verre à la main. 10. Autrefois *il y avait* vingt églises dans cette ville. 11. Guillaume *avait*-il fini son thème? 12. Henriette *avait*-elle appris sa poésie par cœur?

54.

1. The Romans had a large army. 2. Had they not taken a music lesson? 3. Formerly there were seven kings in this country. 4. He had always a great kindness for me. 5. I have found my dog. 6. Where had you sought him? 7. In the meadow. 8. Had you not a French exercise? 9. Was she right or wrong? 10. She was right, but my brothers were wrong. 11. We had five mistakes in our exercise and our cousins had seventeen mistakes. 12. There were fifteen boats on the lake. 13. How many oars had you? 14. We had eight oars?

55.

Imperfect (*Imparfait*) of être, *to be:* —

j'étais, *I was*	étais-je? *was I?* etc.
tu étais, *thou wast*	étais-tu? etc.
il (elle) était, *he (she) was*	je n'étais pas, *I was not,* etc.
nous étions, *we were*	tu n'étais pas, etc.
vous étiez, *you were*	n'étais-je pas? *was I not?* etc.
ils (elles) étaient, *they were.*	n'étais-tu pas? etc.

Practice:— *Put the Auxiliary Verbs in all sentences of Exs. 27 and 29 in the* **Imperfect** *tense.*

le premier, *m.* ⎱ *the first*
la première, *f.* ⎰
les parents, *the parents,*
   the relatives
victorieux, *victorious*
hier (au) soir, *yesterday evening*
Salomon, *Solomon*
gai, *gay, cheerful*
le nom, *the name*
presque, *almost, nearly*
puissant, *powerful*
lorsque, *when*
dites-moi, *tell me*
meilleur, *best.*

1. Hier j'*étais* chez mon oncle. 2. Où *étais*-tu hier matin? 3. Hier matin j'*étais* à l'école. 4. Dans quelle classe *étais*-tu? 5. J'*étais* dans la première classe. 6. Quand nous *avions* encore nos parents, nous *étions* très-heureux. 7. Ton frère *était* mon meilleur ami, nous *étions* toujours gais et contents. 8. Pourquoi n'avez-vous pas suivi mon conseil? 9. Parce qu'il *n'était pas* bon. 10. Les Romains *étaient* presque toujours victorieux. 11. Pourquoi *n'étiez*-vous *pas* les premiers de la classe? 12. Parce que nous n'avions pas étudié. 13. Rome *était* autrefois très puissante. 14. Quels sont les noms français des jours de la semaine?

56.

1. Last week I was in London, and my brother was in Paris. 2. Your brother William was formerly my friend, but now he is my enemy. 3. Napoleon was emperor of the French. 4. David and Solomon were kings of the Jews. 5. Where were you yesterday evening? 6. We were in the capital of France. 7. Were you not tired? 8. No, we were not tired. 9. Was he not wrong? 10. Was not your sister ill yesterday? 11. Yes, she and her cousin were very ill and sad. 12. Why was she so pale? 13. Was not the window open? 14. The *Palais-Royal* belonged (was) formerly to the king Louis-Philippe. 15. Why were the doors not shut? 16. Because the windows were shut.

NUMERALS.

57.

21, vingt et un	41, quarante et un,	77, soixante-dix-sept
22, vingt-deux	etc.	78, soixante-dix-huit
23, vingt-trois	50, cinquante	79, soixante-dix-neuf
24, vingt-quatre	60, soixante	80, quatre-vingts
25, vingt-cinq	69, soixante-neuf	81, quatre-vingt-un
26, vingt-six	70, soixante-dix	82, quatre-vingt-deux,
27, vingt-sept	71, soixante-onze	etc.
28, vingt-huit	72, soixante-douze	90, quatre-vingt-dix
29, vingt-neuf	73, soixante-treize	91, quatre-vingt-onze
30, trente	74, soixante-quatorze	100, cent
31, trente et un, etc.	75, soixante-quinze	101, cent (et) un
40, quarante	76, soixante-seize	200, deux cents

250, deux cent cinquante   2000, deux mille (no s)
300, trois cents, etc.   1,000,000, un million
1000, mille (in dates mil)   2,000,000, deux millions
1872, mil huit cent soixante-douze.

le bon point, *the mark*   la dent, *the tooth*   avant-dernier, *last but one*
l'élève, *m. & f. the pupil*   le schelling, *the shilling*   vaut, *is worth* (Inf. valoir)
la livre, *the pound*   le centime, *the cent*   valent, *are worth*
l'heure, *f. the hour*   le sou, *the sou, halfpenny*   environ, *about*
la minute, *the minute*   demi, *half*   à peu près, *nearly*
la seconde*, *the second*   (*c *pronounced like* g.)   le jardinier, *the gardener.*

1. N'aviez-vous pas *vingt et un* bons points? 2. Non, monsieur, j'avais *trente-neuf* bons points. 3. Combien d'élèves étiez-vous dans votre école? 4. Nous étions *cinquante-cinq* élèves. 5. Combien vaut *une* livre sterling? 6. *Une* livre sterling vaut *vingt-cinq* francs. 7. Combien de francs valent *deux* livres sterling? 8. Combien de florins valent *trois* livres sterling? 9. L'heure a *soixante* minutes, et la minute a *soixante* secondes . 10. Un franc vaut *vingt* sous. 11. Combien de sous *valent* deux francs et demi? 12. L'homme a *trente-deux* dents. 13. Un franc vaut à peu près *dix* pence et un penny vaut *dix* centimes. 14. Combien font *trois* fois *dix-sept? quatre* fois *quinze? cinq* fois *treize? six* fois *six?*

58.

1. How many are 3×23, 6×11, 7×9, 3×23, 4×12, 5×8, 2×29? 2. How many days are there in this month? 3. There are thirty days, but last month there were thirty-one days, and in the last but one twenty-eight days. 4. How many hours are there in two days and [a] half; how many minutes in this hours? 5. How many shillings are two pounds sterling. 6. Four shillings are worth five francs. 7. How many francs are 16, 24, 32, 48, 52 shillings. 8. This French book is worth two francs.

59.

janvier, *m. January*
février, *m. February*
mars, *m. March*
avril, *m. April*
mai, *m. May*
juin, *m. June*
juillet, *m. July*
août (a mute), *m. August*
septembre, *m. September*
octobre, *m. October*
novembre, *m. November*
décembre, *m. December*
le grand-père, *the grandfather*
la grand' mère, *the grandmother*

l'habitant, *m. the inhabitant*
le comté, *the county*
le comte, *the count, earl*
le compte, *the account*
le conte, *the tale*
lorsque, *when*
né, (Past Part. of naître) *born*
ordinaire, *ordinary*
bissextile, *leap (year)*
suivant, *following*
Bruxelles, *Brussels*
l'âge, *m. the age*   Anvers, *Antwerp*
la Nouvelle Orléans, *New Orleans*
plus que (de), *more than.*

Quel âge avez-vous?   *How old are you?*
J'ai quinze ans   *I am fifteen years old.*

1. Mon grand-père a *quatre-vingt-dix-neuf* ans. 2. Quel âge votre grand' mère avait-elle, lorsqu'elle était chez vous? 3. Elle avait 78 ans. 4. Quand êtes-vous né? 5. Je suis né en janvier *mil huit cent cinquante-cinq*. 6. Quatre fois *vingt* font *quatre-vingts*. 7. *Deux* fois *quarante et un* font *quatre-vingt-deux*. 8. Combien de jours a l'année ordinaire? 9. Combien de jours a l'année bissextile? 10. Combien d'habitants y a-t-il dans les villes suivantes: Lyon, Bruxelles, Douvres, Anvers, La Nouvelle Orléans? 11. Combien font *quatre-vingt-dix-huit* moins *vingt-deux?* 12. L'année a *douze* mois: janvier, février, mars, avril, mai, juin, juillet, août, septembre, octobre, novembre, décembre. 13. La France a 36 millions d'habitants.

60.

Pronounce in French:— 222, 365, 499, 501, 678, 789, 861, 936, 1872, 2488, 15, 815, 24,999. $3 \times 71 = 213$, $5 \times 82 = 410$. $691 - 108 = 583$. $388 + 410 = 798$.

1. How old was your grandfather in January? 2. He was 91 years old, and in July my grandmother was 89 years old. 3. How many days are there in the months of February, April and May? 4. How many counties are there in England? 5. When was (is) your brother born? 6. He was born in August 1849. 7. A French mètre is more than* three feet. 8. There are 69 boys in this class. 9. Berlin has now more than* 600,000 inhabitants. 10. [One] hundred pounds sterling are two thousand five hundred francs.

*de.

61.

Avoir, — Preterite (*Passé Défini*). — **Être,**

j'eus, *I had*	je fus, *I was*
tu eus, *thou hadst*	tu fus, *thou wast*
il (elle) eut, *he (she) had*	il (elle) fut, *he (she) was*
nous eûmes, *we had*	nous fûmes, *we were*
vous eûtes, *you had*	vous fûtes, *you were*
ils (elles) eurent, *they had.*	ils (elles) furent, *they were.*

On the difference between the **Imperfect** and **Preterite**, see *Eugène's Comparative French Grammar*, § 135.

la visite, *the visit, call*
la pension, *the boarding-school*
l'inventeur, *the inventor*
l'imprimerie, *f. the printing*
la quantité, *the quantity*
fixé, *fixed*
nommé, *called*
le conquérant, *the conqueror*
ne .. que, *only*
la leçon de français, *the French lesson*
la leçon d'écriture, *the writing lesson*
la géographie, *Geography*
Azincourt, *Agincourt*
mal à la tête, *head ache*
mal aux dents, *tooth ache*
être enrhumé, *to have a cold*
plusieurs, *several*
surpris, *surprised*
tué, *killed*
beaucoup de, *many, much.*

1. *N'eûtes*-vous *pas* hier la visite de votre ami Albert? 2. Oui, monsieur, j'*eus* sa visite. 3. Charles *n'eut-il pas* beaucoup de fautes dans son thème? 4. Non, il *n'eut que* trois fautes. 5. *N'eûmes*-nous *pas* raison? 6. Non, mes amis, vous *eûtes* tort. 7. Où le roi Richard fut-il tué? 8. *Ne fûtes*-vous *pas* très fatigués? 9. Combien de leçons d'allemand *eûtes*-vous la semaine dernière? 10. Vos cousines *eurent*-elles un maître de musique? 11. Combien de temps vos sœurs *furent*-elles à la pension? 12. Qui *fut* l'inventeur de l'imprimerie? 13. C'est Guttemberg qui *fut* l'inventeur de l'imprimerie. 14. Dites-moi les noms français des mois de l'année? 15. Qu'*eûtes*-vous? 16. Je *fus* enrhumé. 17. J'*eus* mal à la tête. 18. *Eûtes*-vous mal aux dents?

62.

1. Romulus was the first king of Rome. 2. Last year we had a large quantity of pears and apples. 3. Were you not very much surprised? 4. Last week I had three music lessons. 5. What lessons had you in (the) school? 6. We had a writing lesson, a French lesson and a lesson in* Geography. 7. Had they a letter from Antwerp or from Brussels this morning? 8. They had two letters from Dover. 9. Were they not satisfied? 10. Was not (the) king William called the conqueror. 11. Had he not several sons? 12. Were the English victorious in the battle of Agincourt?

63.

Future (*Futur*) of Avoir, *to have.*

j'aurai, *I shall have* | je n'aurai pas, *I shall not have,*
tu auras, *thou wilt have* | tu n'auras pas, etc.
il (elle) aura, *he (she) will have*
on aura, *one will have* | aurai-je, *shall I have? etc.*
nous aurons, *we shall have* | auras-tu? etc.
vous aurez, *you will have* | n'aurai-je pas? *shall I not have?*
ils (elles) auront, *they will have* | n'auras-tu pas? etc.

Compare the terminations of the Future with the Pres. Tense of avoir.

le plaisir, *the pleasure*   le manteau, *the cloak*   trop, *too, too much, too*
peu (de), *few, little, (adv.)*   sage, rangé, *orderly*   *many*
le neveu, *the nephew*   l'après-midi, *f. the after-*   prochain, *near, next*
la nièce, *the niece*   *noon*   avoir faim, *to be hungry*
l'assiduité, *f. the industry*   demain, *to-morrow*   avoir soif, *to be thirsty.*
les devoirs, *m.* {*the duties*   après-demain, *the day*
{*the lesson*   *after to-morrow*

From Ex. 26 and 30 form 12 sentences with avoir in the **Future** *and with appropriate adverbs: as,* **demain** *instead of* **hier,** *etc.*

1. N'*aurai*-je pas ce plaisir? 2. Oui, mon ami, tu *auras* ce plaisir demain. 3. Il *aura* faim quand il aura pris un bain. 4. Votre ami Jean *aura*-t-il un prix? 5. Oui, il *aura* un prix, s'il est appliqué. 6. *Aurons*-nous la visite de notre neveu? 7. Oui, madame, vous *aurez* demain la visite de mon neveu et de ma nièce. 8. Y *aura*-t-il beaucoup de fruit cette année? 9. Non, il y *aura* peu de fruit. 10. Les Français *auront*-ils la paix ou la guerre? 11. Ils *auront* la paix; ils ont eu la guerre assez longtemps. 12. Il *aura* faim et soif ce soir. 13. N'*aurez*-vous pas froid dans cet habit d'été? 14. N'*aura*-t-il pas chaud avec ce manteau? 15. Non, il n'*aura* pas trop chaud.

64.

1. [The] next[2] week[1] I shall have two writing lessons, but I shall not have a drawing lesson. 2. You will have (Sing.) a reward for your industry. 3. The day after to-morrow my nephew will have his writing book, his pencil, his pen and his inkstand. 4. Your nieces will be hungry and thirsty. 5. To-morrow you will have a fine day. 6. Next Monday we shall have a holiday. 7. Why? Because we have been very industrious and orderly. 8. Shall you have a music lesson [on] Thursday? 9. No, we shall not have a music lesson, but we shall have a German lesson on Friday.

FUTURE OF ÊTRE.

65.
Future (*Futur*) of **être**, *to be*.

je serai, *I shall be*
tu seras, *thou wilt be*
il (elle) sera, *he (she) will be*
on sera, *one will be*
nous serons, *we shall be*
vous serez, *you will be*
ils (elles) seront, *they will be*

je ne serai pas, *I shall not be, etc.*
tu ne seras pas, etc.

serai-je *Shall I be?* etc.
seras-tu? etc.

ne serai-je pas? *Shall I not be?*
ne seras-tu pas? etc.

For practice form 12 sentences from Exs. 45 & 46 with the verb être *in the* Future *and substitute appropriate Adverbs: as,*
la semaine prochaine, demain, *instead of* la semaine dernière, hier, etc.

la Belgique, *Belgium*
belge, *Belgian*
la route, *the road, way*
en route, *on the way*
Jacques, *James*
les vacances, *f. the vacations*
du monde, *company*
la fête, *the feast, holyday*

certainement, *certainly*
la société, *the society*
midi, *twelve o'clock (noon)*
minuit, „ *(midnight)*
l'esclave, *m. & f. the slave*
obtenu, *obtained, got*
ne ... point de, *not any*
donc,*then;* alors,*then*(referring *to* time).

1. Où *seras*-tu demain, mon ami? 2. Je *serai* demain matin à Paris. 3. Et où *sera* ton frère Jacques? 4. Mon frère Jacques *sera* en route pour la Belgique. 5. Quand *sera*-t-il à Bruxelles? 6. Il *sera* à Bruxelles à trois heures du soir et à Cologne à huit heures du matin. 7. Quand-*serez* vous contents? 8. Nous *serons* contents quand nous aurons nos habits neufs. 9. Combien *serez*-vous dans votre classe après les vacances? 10. Nous *serons* quarante-quatre. 11. Votre cousine *sera*-t-elle heureuse, quand elle *sera* à la maison? 12. Oui, elle *sera* très contente. 13. Il n'y *aura* point de fêtes cette semaine. 14. A quel jour a-t-il fixé son départ? — A vendredi matin. 15. A quelle heure *seront*-ils à Milan? — A midi.

66.
1. When shall you be satisfied[1] then[2]? 2. When I (shall) have obtained the first prize. 3. Will my cousin Alice have company to-morrow evening? 4. No, she will not have company. 5. Will not the soldiers be too tired? 6. Will your father also be of our company? 7. Wilt thou be at home [on] Wednesday next? 8. Will our master be satisfied with (of) our exercises? 9. He will certainly be satisfied, if there are no mistakes. 10. At what o'clock will you be in school to-day, my dear little friend?

67.

Avoir: Conditional (*Conditionnel*).   **Être:**

1. j'aurais, *I should have*
tu aurais, *thou wouldst have*
il (elle) aurait, *he (she) would have*
nous aurions, *we should have*
vous auriez, *you would have*
ils (elles) auraient, *they would have*.

je serais, *I should be*
tu serais, *thou wouldst be*
il (elle) serait, *he (she) would be*
nous serions, *we should be*
vous seriez, *you would be*
ils (elles) seraient, *they would be*.

Compare the inflections of the Conditional with the Imperfect of avoir.

je n'aurais pas, etc., *I should not have, etc.*
aurais-je? etc., *should I have? etc.*
n'aurais-je pas? etc., *should I not have? etc.*

je ne serais pas; etc., *I should not be, etc.*
serais-je? *should I be? etc.*
ne serais-je pas? etc., *should I not be? etc.*

le général, *the general*
les troupes, *f. the troops*
la promenade, *the walk*
sans, *without, but for*
économe, *economical, saving*
la complaisance, } *the kindness*
la bonté, }
tranquille, *quiet*

mécontent, *dissatisfied*
marché, *marched, walked*
prudent, *prudent, cautious*
charmé, *delighted*
occupé, *occupied*
si, (conjunction) *if, whether*
si, (adverb) *so*
voyagé, *travelled*.

1. Ma sœur *serait* contente, si elle avait ces fleurs. 2. J'*aurais* tort, si j'étais mécontent. 3. *Auriez*-vous fait cela? 4. Oui, j'*aurais* fait cela, si j'avais eu le temps. 5. Votre nièce *aurait*-elle raison, si elle avait donné son argent? 6. Non, elle *n'aurait* pas eu raison. 7. Le général *serait*-il victorieux, s'il avait assez de troupes? 8. Si Émile était appliqué, *aurait*-il vingt fautes dans son thème? 9. *N'auriez*-vous *pas* faim, si vous aviez marché? 10. Oui, nous *aurions* faim et soif. 11. Votre voisin *ne serait*-il pas riche, s'il avait été économe? 12. Cela *serait*-il vrai?

68.

1. I should have taken (made) a walk, if the weather had been fine. 2. You would be wrong. 3. They would be right. 4. But for your kindness we should be very unhappy. 5. My nephew would not be so ill, if he had been more cautious. 6. Our neighbour would be rich, if he were less prodigal. 7. We should be in London to-morrow, if we were not so busy. 8. We should be hungry and thirsty if we had walked so long. 9. They would be cold if they were in that country. 10. You would be warm if you had a cloak. 11. Would you have this kindness?

69.

-ill- *in the middle, and* -il *at the end of a word, generally have what is called a* liquid *sound (to be learned from the master)*:—

bouteille, conseilla, bataille, travailler, paille, famille, fille, feuille;

soleil, éveil, orgueil, œil, détail, travail, brillant.

Obs. The vowels a and i in -ail and -aille do not form a diphthong; the a must be sounded separately:—

bataille, *pronounce* bata-ye.
travail, „ trava-ye.

le papier, *the paper*	la feuille, *the leaf, sheet (of paper)*	travaillé, *worked*
le soleil, *the sun*		brillant, *brilliant*
la bouteille, *the bottle*	le feuillet, *the leaf (of a book)*	éveillé, *awakened, awake*
la paille, *the straw*		cueilli, *culled, gathered*
la famille, *the family*	le tailleur, *the tailor*	mouillé, *wet, wetted*
l'orgueil, *m. the pride, haughtiness*	joué, *played*	couvert, *covered, cloudy*
	le garçon, *the boy, waiter, the bachelor*	sale, *soiled, dirty*
la fille, *the daughter*		

1. As-tu travaillé ce matin? 2. Oui, j'ai travaillé et joué. 3. Le soleil était brillant hier matin. 4. Où sont les bouteilles? 5. Les bouteilles sont sur la paille. 6. Avez-vous vu sa famille? 7. Oui, mademoiselle, j'ai vu sa famille. 8. Il est sans orgueil. 9. Est-il éveillé? 10. Le tailleur a apporté votre gilet. 11. Où sont vos filles à présent? 12. Elles sont à l'école. 13. Où as-tu cueilli ces fleurs? 14. J'ai cueilli ces fleurs dans la prairie. 15. Pourquoi as-tu mouillé la feuille? 16. Les feuillets de votre livre sont sales. 17. Voici une feuille de papier.

70.

In this Exercise answer in French all the sentences which are interrogative.

1. Have you worked or played this morning? 2. Were the stars bright last evening? 3. Have the waiters filled the bottles? 4. Will your family be in Edinburgh next week? 5. Where were their daughters and nieces last Thursday? 6. Are the leaves of the trees not green? 7. Have you not two sheets of this paper? 8. Has the gardener gathered the fruit? 9. The sun would be very bright this morning, if the sky were not so cloudy. 10. The sun is the eye of the world. 11. Would you have this kindness? 12. Would my niece not be delighted, if she had this veil?

71.

gn *has a liquid sound (to be learned from the master):*—
agneau, compagnon, espagnol, Champagne, signe, gagné, Cologne, Allemagne, soigner, cigogne, Pologne.

la Pologne, *Poland*	la province, *the province*
l'Espagne, *f. Spain*	le compagnon, *m.* ⎫ *the companion*
l'Allemagne, *f. Germany*	la compagne, *f.* ⎭ *the mate*
la Champagne, *Champagne*	défendu, *defended, forbidden*
la campagne, *the country*	la différence, *the difference*
la Bretagne, *Brittany*	le royaume, *the kingdom*
la Grande-Bretagne, *Great Britain*	digne, *worthy*
l'Écosse, *f. Scotland*	entre, *between*
l'Irlande, *f. Ireland*	uni, *united, smooth*
la vigne, *the vine, vineyard*	catholique, *Catholic*
le terme, *the term*	protestant, *Protestant*
le fermier, *the farmer*	situé, *situated*
le citoyen, *the citizen*	l'Espagnol, *the Spaniard*
la montagne, *the mountain*	forment (3ᵈ p. pl.) *form.*

Obs. *Names of countries ending in* e *mute are feminine.*

1. Avez-vous été en Pologne? 2. Non, monsieur, mais j'ai été en Allemagne et dans la Grande-Bretagne. 3. Les Espagnols sont-ils catholiques ou protestants? 4. Votre compagnon est-il à Cologne? 5. Non, mademoiselle, il est à Boulogne. 6. Il y a beaucoup de vignes en Espagne et en Champagne. 7. Votre nièce est-elle à la campagne? 8. Oui, madame, elle est partie hier avec sa campagne. 9. Quelle différence y a-t-il entre les termes *pays, patrie* et *campagne?* 10. Les citoyens ont défendu leur patrie. 11. La Russie est un grand pays. 12. Le fermier n'est pas dans la ville, mais à la campagne. 13. L'Angleterre, l'Écosse et l'Irlande forment le Royaume-Uni de Grande-Bretagne.

72.

1. Is he worthy of that reward? 2. How many pounds has he earned? 3. In what country is Cologne situated? In Germany. 4. Is your companion in the town or in the country? 5. England is the native country of Nelson. 6. Would they be in the country, if the weather was fine? 7. Brittany is a province of France. 8. Ireland is a part of Great Britain. Great Britain is more powerful than Spain. 9. Have you travelled in the mountains of Scotland? 10. You would not be so unhappy, my dear companions, if you were not so dissatisfied.

73.] Avoir: Imperative.   Être:
aie, *have thou*   sois, *be thou*
ayons, *let us have*   soyons, *let us be*
ayez, *have ye*   soyez, *be ye.*
ti *sounds like* ssi *or* cy (*as:* mer*cy):—*
ti *sounds like* ti *hard (as* Engl. *tea):—*
1) in the terminations tial, tiel, tieux:— partial, essentiel, ambitieux.
1) in the terminations tié, tier, tième:— amitié, moitié, portier, huitième.
2) in tion (if not preceded by s, x):— action, consolation, révolution.
2) in tion preceded by s or x:— question, mixtion.
3) in tie:— prophétie, aristocratie, Helvétie.
3) in tie (if the feminine of ti):— partie, bâtie, sortie.
4) in tien of proper nouns: vénitien, helvétien.
4) in tien of common nouns:— le tien, je tiens, le maintien.

Most Substantives ending in tion, tié, tie, té are feminine. (See Eugène's Comp. French Gram. § 113.)

la prononciation, *the pronunciation*
l'Helvétie, *f. Helvetia*
l'Helvétien, *m. the Helvetian*
l'amitié, *f. the friendship*
la chose, *the thing*
le bagage, *the luggage, baggage*
la consolation, { *the consolation*
                 { *the comfort*
l'affliction, *f. the affliction*

la Suisse, *Switzerland*
la révolution, *the revolution*
la question, *the question*
ambitieux, *ambitious*
précieux, *precious*
correct, *correct*
essentiel, *essential*
éclaté, *burst out*
abandonné, *abandoned.*

1. La prononciation anglaise est-elle difficile? 2. Oui, elle est très difficile. 3. Napoléon était très ambitieux. 4. Helvétie est l'ancien nom pour la Suisse. 5. Août est le huitième mois de l'année. 6. La vraie amitié est une chose précieuse. 7. Le portier a-t-il apporté mon bagage? 8. L'amitié est une consolation dans les afflictions. 9. Une prononciation correcte est essentielle.

74.

1. Where has he learnt his German pronunciation? 2. The Helvetians had abandoned their native country. 3. He is not worthy of your friendship. 4. This question is essential. 5. He has not understood my question. 6. The history of the English Revolution is very interesting. 7. Cromwell was very ambitious. 8. Your friendship is my consolation. 9. Let us have a good book. 10. Be [thou] prudent. 11. Be [ye] satisfied.

75.
ORDINAL NUMBERS.

le premier, \} *the first*
la première,

le second, la seconde,[1] *the second*
le (la) deuxième,[2] „
le troisième, *the third*
le quatrième, *the fourth*
le cinquième, *the fifth*
[3]le huitième, *the eighth*
le neuvième, *the ninth*

le dixième, *the tenth*
[3]le onzième, *the eleventh*
le vingtième, *the twentieth*
le vingt et unième, *the 21st*
le vingt-deuxième, *the 22d*
le trentième, *the thirtieth*
le centième, *the hundredth*
le dernier, la dernière, *the last*
l'avant-dernier, *the last but one.*

[1]pronounce c = g.   [2]x = z.   [3]e not elided.

le rang, *the rank, place*
les mathématiques, *f. mathematics*
la honte, *the shame*
avoir honte, *to be ashamed*
le successeur, *the successor*
Henri, *Henry*
Édouard, *Edward*

Jean, *John*
Noël, *m., Christmas*
paresseux, *idle*
honteux, *shameful, ashamed*
fi donc! *for shame!*
tant mieux! *so much the better!*

quel quantième, *which day of the month?*
le congé, *the holiday*
mort, *(adj.) dead*
la mort, *death*
né, *born*
Frédéric, *Frederick.*

Cardinal *Numbers are used in French instead of* **Ordinal** *with the names of* **Sovereigns** *and the* **days** *of the month, except the first:—*

François premier, *Francis the first;*
Henri deux, *Henry the second;*
Louis quatorze, *Louis the fourteenth;*

le premier mai, *the first of May*
le deux juin, *June the 2nd*
le vingt et un février, *February the 21st.*

1. Es-tu le *premier* de la classe? 2. Non, monsieur, je suis le *vingt et unième.* 3. Quel est ton rang en classe, mon fils? 4. Je suis à présent le *deuxième* en latin, et le *neuvième* en mathématiques. 5. Et en français? 6. En français je suis le *onzième.* 7. Comment, le *onzième?* mais, n'étais-tu pas le *premier?* 8. Oui, mon père, l'année *dernière* j'étais le *premier.*

76.

1. Henry is the first in (of) his class, Charles the second, Edward the fifth, Frederick the eleventh, John the twenty-first, Alfred the last but one, and James the last. 2. Which is your place in mathematics? 3. I am the thirtieth. 4. That is disgraceful; for shame, you idle fellow! 5. What day of the month have we to-day. 6. To-day is the 31st of March. 7. To-morrow is the first of April. 8. [On] the first of next month we shall have a holiday. 9. So much the better! 10. James was born [on] the 21st of June 1851.

77.

Avoir: Future Past (*Futur Passé*).   Être:

j'aurai eu, *I shall have had,*	j'aurai été, *I shall have been,*
tu auras eu *etc.*	tu auras été *etc.*
il aura eu	il aura été
nous aurons eu	nous aurons été
vous aurez eu	vous aurez été
ils auront eu.	ils auront été.

Observe the following use of the Future Past, to express **probability** *or* **supposition**: —

Pourquoi n'est-il pas venu?	*Why did he not come?* —
Il **aura** été malade.	*He* **probably has been** *ill.*

y, *there*
pendant, *during*
l'édition, *f. the edition*
tard, *late*

le boulanger, *the baker*
l'autre, *the other*
un (une) autre, *another*
le pharmacien, *the chemist.*

1. Adolphe est venu deux heures trop tard. 2. Où *aura*-t-il *été* pendant ce temps? 3. Il *aura été* à l'école. 4. Pourquoi le maître n'est-il pas venu? 5. Il *n'aura pas eu* le temps. 6. Serez-vous à Lyon demain? 7. Non, pas demain, mais nous y serons après-demain, et samedi prochain nous *aurons* déjà *été* à Marseille. 8. Pourquoi n'ont-ils pas acheté du pain blanc? 9. Le boulanger *n'aura* eu *que* du pain noir. 10. Quel roi fut le successeur de Henri trois de France? — Ce fut Henri quatre. 11. Et qui fut le successeur de Henri quatre? — Louis treize.

78.

1. Why has your nephew bought this edition of Shakespeare? 2. The bookseller [probably] had not (Fut. past) another edition. 3. Why did (is) he not come? 4. He [probably] has not had time. 5. Will they have been at school? 6. They will have been at church. 7. Will they have had (the) time? 8. They will not have had time. 9. He died (is dead) this morning. 10. Christmas is always on the 25th of December. 11. Henry the Eigth died on the 28th of January 1547.

79.

Avoir: Conditional Past (*Conditionnel Passé*). **Être:**

j'aurais eu, *I should have*	j'aurais été, *I should have*
tu aurais eu *had, etc.*	tu aurais été *been, etc.*
il aurait eu	il aurait été
nous aurions eu	nous aurions été
vous auriez eu	vous auriez été
ils auraient eu.	ils auraient été.

Aurais-je eu? etc. *Should I* ⎫
Je n'aurais pas eu, *I should not* ⎬ *have*
N'aurais-je pas eu? *Should I not* ⎭ *had;*

Aurais-je été? *Should I* ⎫
Je n'aurais pas été, *I should not* ⎬ *have*
N'aurais-je pas été? *Should I not* ⎭ *been;*

For practice conjugate in all persons sing. and plur.:—
J'aurais eu le premier prix, si j'avais été appliqué,

la distance,* *the distance*
le théâtre, *the theatre*
le danger, *the danger*
la pitié, *the pity*
la bataille, *the battle*
l'avantage, *m. the advantage*
tant de, *so many*

humain, *human, humane*
imprudent, *imprudent, rash*
la récompense,* *the reward*
la compagnie, *the company*
l'examen, *m. the examination*
indisposé, *unwell*
le malheur, *the misfortune.*

*Substantives ending in -ence, -ance are feminine, except le silence.

1. J'aurais eu beaucoup de plaisir à la campagne, si le temps avait été beau. 2. J'aurais été au concert, si je n'avais pas été indisposé. 3. *N'auraient*-ils *pas eu* pitié de ces malheureux, s'ils avaient été humains? 4. *N'aurait*-il *pas eu* le premier prix, s'il avait travaillé? 5. *N'auraient*-ils *pas été* charmés de votre visite? 6. Nous *aurions été* en grand danger, si les ennemis avaient gagné la bataille. 7. Vous *auriez eu* un grand avantage sur nous, si vous aviez eu le premier prix. 8. Vous *auriez été* bien imprudent, si vous étiez parti avec lui. 9. Nous *n'aurions pas eu* cet argent sans votre complaisance. 10. S'ils avaient été appliqués, ils *n'auraient pas eu* tant de fautes.

80.

1. We should have had much pleasure in Paris, if we had had a friend in that large city. 2. If we had been at home we should have had the pleasure (of) [to] be in his company. 3. Would you have friends, if you were not so rich? 4. If the master had had (the) time, the examination would have taken place. 5. They would have been very unhappy. 6. Would you not have had pity on* this man, if you had known his misfortune? 7. Yes we should have had pity on* him. 8. You would not have been in danger if you had not been imprudent.

81.
THE FIRST CONJUGATION.

comprises all Verbs ending in -er *in the Infinitive.*

Infinitive:— parl-**er,** *to speak*
Present Participle:— parl-**ant,** *speaking*
Past Participle:— parl-**é,** *spoken.*

For the Formation of Tenses from the Principal Parts see Appendix.

Present Indicative:—

je parle,   *I speak, I am speaking, I do speak,*
tu parles,   *thou speakest, thou art speaking,*
il (elle) parle, *he (she) speaks, he (she) is speaking,*
on parle,   *one speaks, one is speaking,*
nous parlons, *we speak, we are speaking,*
vous parlez, *you speak, you are speaking,*
ils (elles) parlent, *they speak, they are speaking.*

Imperative:—

Sing.	Plur.
1. — — —	parlons, *let us speak*
2. parle, *speak thou*	parlez, *speak ye*
3. qu'il, elle parle, *let him, her speak*	qu'ils parlent, *let them speak.*

Je ne parle pas, *I do not speak;* or *I am not speaking,*
tu ne parles pas, etc.
Parlé*-je? *Do I speak?* or *Am I speaking?* etc.
parles-tu? etc.
Ne parlé*-je pas? *Do I not speak?* or *Am I not speaking?*
ne parles-tu pas? etc.   *See Observation below.

A verb may also be made interrogative by putting **est-ce que** (literally "**is it that**") before the affirmative:—

Do I speak? etc.	*Do we speak? etc.*
Est-ce que je parle?	Est-ce que nous parlons?
est-ce que tu parles?	est-ce que vous parlez?
est-ce qu'il parle?	est-ce qu'ils parlent?
est-ce qu'elle parle?	est-ce qu'elles parlent?

Est-ce que je ne parle pas? etc. *Do I not speak? etc.*

Obs. This latter construction is preferred especially in the 1ˢᵗ p. sing. Prest. Indic. of many verbs for the sake of euphony:—

Est-ce que je corrige? *instead of* Corrigé-je?
Est-ce que je vends?   „   vends-je?

THE FIRST CONJUGATION.

To be conjugated like parler:—
trouver, *to find*
aimer, *to love*
fermer, *to shut, close*
montrer, *to show*
travailler, *to work*
donner, *to give.*

Practice:— je parle français,
tu parles italien,
il parle espagnol, etc.

je ne parle pas mal,
tu ne parles pas haut,
il ne parle pas bien, etc.

le chapeau, *the hat, bonnet*
le piano, *the piano*
mademoiselle, *Miss*
la demoiselle, *the young lady*
la carte, *the card, map*
correctement, *correctly*
distinctement, *distinctly*
eh bien! *well!*
ce qui (Subject) } *that which,*
ce que (Object) } *what*
de bonne heure, *early*
au lieu de, *instead of*

jouer de, *to play* (a musical instrument)
jouer à, *to play* (at a game)
chanter, *to sing*
étudier, *to study*
commencer, *to begin*
honorer, *to honour*
regarder, *to regard, to look (at)*
chercher, *to search, to look (for)*
écouter, *to listen*
babiller, *to chatter*
oublier, *to forget*
apporter, *to bring.*

1. Je *joue* et tu *travailles.* 2. Il *aime* à étudier. 3. *Parlez*-vous anglais, mademoiselle? 4. Non, monsieur, je ne *parle* pas anglais, mais je *parle* allemand. 5. Eh bien, *parlons* un peu allemand. 6. Mes frères *travaillent*, mon cousin *travaille* aussi. 7. Écoutez, le maître *commence* à parler. 8. *Fermez* la porte, et *apportez* les livres. 9. *Regardez* bien! 10. *Écoutons* au lieu de babiller. 11. Mon oncle *joue aux* cartes et mon cousin *joue du* violon. 12. *N'oubliez*-vous pas votre leçon? 13. Non, nous *n'oublions* pas nos leçons. 14. Nous *parlons* correctement et vous *parlez* distinctement. 15. *Est-ce que vous étudiez*, mes élèves? 16. Oui, monsieur, nous *étudions* assidûment. 17. *Est-ce qu'ils n'apportent pas* leurs livres? 18. Non, madame, mais ils *apportent* leurs cahiers. 19. Comment *trouvez*-vous ces pommes? 20. Nous *trouvons* ces pommes excellentes.

82.

1. I speak French to my cousins (f.) and they speak Italian to their sisters. 2. Do they also speak Spanish? 3. No, they do not (speak Spanish). 4. Are you working or playing? 5. We are not playing, we are working. 6. We often[1] forget[2] what we have learnt. 7. Do you not think (find) my hat too small? 8. We esteem and honour a child that honours his father and (his) mother. 9. What do you look [for]? 10. I am looking [for] my dog. 11. You speak very well, but you do not study enough. 12. Is your niece working? 13. No, she is not (working) she is playing on (of) the piano. 14. Let him shut the window and (let him) bring a chair.

POSSESSIVE PRONOUNS.

83.
Possessive Pronouns (*Pronoms Possessifs*).

Singular.			Plural.	
Masc.	*Fem.*		*Masc.*	*Fem.*
le mien,	la mienne,	*mine,*	les miens,	les miennes,
le tien,	la tienne,	*thine,*	les tiens,	les tiennes,
le sien,	la sienne,	*his, hers, its,*	les siens,	les siennes,
le nôtre,	la nôtre,	*ours,*	les nôtres,	
le vôtre,	la vôtre,	*yours,*	les vôtres,	
le leur,	la leur,	*theirs,*	les leurs.	

Observe that in French **Possessive Pronouns** (*like Possessive Adjectives, see Ex. 15*) *agree in* **Gender** *and* **Number** *with the* **Object possessed;** (*and* **not** *with the* **Possessor** *as in English*):

Charles a mon crayon, il a perdu le sien.	Charles *has my pencil, he has lost* his *(own).*
Louise a mon crayon, elle a perdu le sien.	Louisa *has my pencil, she has lost hers.*
Jean a ma plume, il a perdu la sienne.	John *has my pen, he has lost* his.
Émilie a ma plume, elle a perdu la sienne.	Emily *has my pen, she has lost* hers.
Mes amis ont mon livre, ils ont vendu le leur.	My friends *have my book, they have sold* theirs.
Mes amies ont mon livre, elles ont vendu le leur.	My friends *(f.) have my book, they have sold* theirs.
Mes amis ont ma poire, ils ont mangé la leur.	My friends *have my pear, they have eaten* theirs.
Mes amis ont mes plumes et mes crayons, ils n'ont pas trouvé les leurs (m. & f.).	My friends *have taken my pens and pencils, they have not found* theirs.
Elle a mes gants, elle a égaré les siens.	She *has my gloves, she has mislaid* hers.
Il a mes noix, il a mangé les siennes.	He *has my nuts, he has eaten* his *(own) etc.*

Possessive **Pronouns** *must be carefully distinguished from the Possessive* **Adjectives** mon, ma, ton, ta, son, sa, *etc.* (*see Ex. 15*).

POSSESSIVE PRONOUNS.

Mon, ton, son, stand, for the sake of euphony, instead of ma, ta, sa, before feminine substantives beginning with a vowel or silent h:

mon âme, ton habitude, *instead of* ma âme, ma habitude.

le bienfait, *the blessing*	le monument, *the monument*
la carte, *the map, card*	bientôt, *soon*
l'impératrice, *the empress*	ancien, *ancient, old,*
la raison, *the reason*	achevé, *finished*
mais non, *why, no!*	est-ce là? *is that?*
les mœurs, *f. the manners*	sont-ce là? *are those?*
agrandi, *enlarged*	tout à l'heure, *just now, presently.*
la langue, *the tongue, language*	

1. As-tu lu mon livre, Alfred? 2. Oui, mon ami, j'ai lu mon livre et *le tien*. 3. Est-ce là ta plume? 4. Oui, c'est *la mienne*. 5. Est-ce là votre crayon? 6. Mais non, c'est *le vôtre*. 7. Avez-vous écrit votre lettre? 8. Oui, ma sœur; avez-vous aussi écrit *la vôtre?* 9. Est-ce là mon parapluie? 10. Oui, c'est *le tien*. 11. As-tu porté ma lettre à la poste? 12. J'ai porté *la mienne*, mais je n'ai pas vu *la tienne*. 13. Sont-ce là vos bottes? 14. Oui, monsieur, ce sont *les nôtres*. 15. L'impératrice Catherine a agrandi son empire, mais Napoléon a perdu *le sien*. 16. Le portier a-t-il apporté vos bagages? 17. Oui, et il a aussi apporté *les leurs*. 18. Emile a écrit sa lettre, mais Jean n'a pas écrit *la sienne*. 19. Guillaume a fini son thème ce matin, et Jules a commencé *le sien* cette après-midi. 20. Marie aura bientôt achevé son ouvrage, mais Émilie n'a pas encore commencé *le sien*. 21. Sophie cherche sa montre et Julie cherche aussi *la sienne*.

84.

1. Are these your letters or theirs? 2. They (ce) are ours. 3. Am I not thy friend and art thou not mine? 4. Thy sisters and mine would have (be) departed (fem. pl.) if they had not been too late. 5. My sister is of the same age as yours. 6. You have your reasons and I have mine. 7. The manners of (the) ancient nations were very different from (of) ours. 8. Your letters are much longer than mine (sing.). 9. This officer is my friend, is he not also thine? 10. James is bringing his books, but John is not bringing his. 11. Edward is looking [for] his pen, Edward has lost his, and Emily has forgotten hers. 12. The first house in (of) the street is mine, the second is yours, the third is his, and the fourth is theirs. 13. Do you think (find) my garden larger than yours? 14. Yes (Sir), but I find my meadow larger than yours.

FIRST CONJUGATION. 45

85.
Imperfect (*Imparfait*).

je parlais,	*I was speaking, I*	parlais-je?	*was I speaking? etc.*
tu parlais,	*did speak, I used*	parlais-tu?	*etc.*
il parlait,	*to speak, etc.*		*I was not speaking, etc.*
nous parlions,		je ne parlais pas, etc.	
vous parliez,			*Was I not speaking? etc.*
ils parlaient,		ne parlais-je pas? etc.	

Conjugate like "parler" —
penser, *to think*, demeurer, *to reside*, dessiner, *to draw*, danser, *to dance*.
Practice:— je parlais de la guerre, je ne parlais pas du roi,
tu parlais du voisin, etc. tu ne parlais pas à mon ami, etc.

l'étude, *f. the study* de bon appétit, *with good* manger, *to eat*
le Grec (f. Grecque) *the* appétit, *heartily* habiter, *to inhabit*
  Greek la rue, *the street* adorer, *to worship*
Dieu, *m. God* Jeanne, *Jane* brûler, *to burn*
le dieu, *the (heathen) god* absent, *absent* empêcher, *to prevent*
la déesse, *the goddess* sous, *under* vrai, *true* pendant que (conj.) *while*
l'appétit, *m. the appetite* préférer, *to prefer* pendant (prep.) *during*

The following questions to be translated and answered in French:
1. Que *cherchais*-tu tout à l'heure? 2. *Cherchiez*-vous votre crayon ou le mien? 3. *N'aimiez*-vous *pas* à danser, lorsque vous étiez jeune? 4. Pourquoi *préfériez*-vous le français à l'allemand? 5. Dans quelle rue *demeuriez*-vous, lorsque vous étiez à Paris? 6. Qui *habitait* votre maison pendant que vous étiez absents? 7. Quand vous étiez à l'école, *aimiez*-vous l'étude de la géographie? 8. Oui, monsieur et nous *dessinions* souvent des cartes. 9. A quoi *pensais*-tu tout à l'heure? 10. Autrefois tu *aimais* le travail, maintenant tu aimes le jeu. 11. Les Romains *brûlaient* leurs morts. 12. Pendant que nous *jouions*, ils *travaillaient*.

86.
1. Charles was looking for his friends, and Alice was looking for hers. 2. The ancient Greeks and Romans adored (used to adore) a great number of gods and goddesses. 3. Were you not looking [for] your hat just now? 4. Why did you not study when you were young? 5. Because I was often ill, I often[2] had[1] the head-ache. 6. Yet you used to eat very heartily. 7. That is true, but the head-ache did not prevent the appetite. 8. When they were in Germany, they used to sing with their friends. 9. The sisters were playing the piano, and the brothers were listening. 10. What language did the ancient Romans speak? 11. They used to speak (the) Latin.

FIRST CONJUGATION.

87.
Preterite (*Passé Défini*).

je parlai, *I spoke* etc.	parlai-je? *did I speak?* etc.
tu parlas	parlais-tu? etc.
il parla	*I did not speak*, etc.
nous parlâmes	je ne parlai pas, etc.
vous parlâtes	*Did I not speak?* etc.
ils parlèrent.	ne parlai-je pas? etc.

Conjugate like "parler" —

quitter, *to leave*
visiter, *to visit*
la chanson, *the song*
le chemin de fer, *the railway*
la Grèce, *Greece*
Tarquin, *Tarquinius*
Néron, *Nero*
le lendemain, *on the following day*
chemin faisant (pron. ai = e), *on the way*
la gare, *the railway station*

continuer, *to continue*
commander, *to command*
aussitôt que, *as soon as*
déjeuner, *to breakfast*
aller (irr.), *to go*
sonner, *to ring, to strike (clock)*,
frapper, *to strike, to beat*
chasser, *to expel, to hunt*
neiger, *to snow*
fonder, *to found*.

remporter, *to carry off*
retourner, *to return*.

The English preposition **on** before dates is not translated in French.

1. Nous *arrivâmes* assez tôt pour déjeuner. 2. Fûtes-vous hier au soir au théâtre? 3. Non, nous ne fûmes pas au théâtre, mais nous fûmes au concert, où Madame Malibran *chanta* une belle chanson. 4. Nous *quittâmes* le concert à dix heures. 5. Aussitôt que nous eûmes déjeuné, nous *allâmes* à l'école. 6. Nous *arrivâmes* à la gare du chemin de fer à neuf heures du matin. 7. Aussitôt que mes frères *arrivèrent* à Londres, ils *visitèrent* l'exposition. 8. Quel roi *remporta* la victoire de Crécy? 9. Quel général *commanda* les Anglais contre le roi Théodore? 10. Qui *fonda* la ville de Rome? 11. Dieu *créa* l'univers.

88.

1. Yesterday evening I studied my lesson and then I drew a head. 2. As soon as they had breakfasted they visited the town. 3. The Romans expelled (the) king Tarquinius and founded a republic. 4. Were you at the railway station yesterday? 5. Which Roman[2] emperor[1] burned Rome? Nero. 6. Did Xerxes continue the war, when he had lost the battle of Salamis? 7. No, he did not continue the war, but he left Greece and returned to (en) Asia. 8. Last[1] Friday[1] we left the town and visited the country. 9. On the following day we continued our journey. 10. On Sunday we visited the cathedral, and on Monday we returned home.

89.

Positive.	Comparative.	Superlative.
grand grande } great grands grandes	plus grand plus grande } greater plus grands plus grandes	le plus grand la plus grande } the greatest les plus grands les plus grandes

The Comparison *of* Superiority *is formed by putting* plus (*more*) *before the* Positive, *and the* Superlative *by putting the definite article before the* Comparative.

The Comparison *of* Inferiority *is expressed by* moins, *that of* Equality *by* aussi, si: —

grand, *great;* moins grand, *(less great), not so great;* le moins grand, *the least;* aussi grand, *as great;* pas si (aussi) grand, *not so great.*

Le plus grand pays, *or* Le pays le plus grand, *The largest country.*

Obs. In *after Superlatives is generally translated by* de (*of*).

le Rhin, *the Rhine*
l'Europe, *f. Europe*
l'Asie, *f. Asia*
l'Afrique, *f. Africa*
l'Australie, *f. Australia*
l'Amérique, *f. America*
l'Égypte, *f. Egypt*
les Alpes, *f. the Alps*

les Pyrénées, *f. the Pyrenees*
généreux, *generous*
que (after comparisons) *than*
le silence, *the silence*
la nuit, *the night*
le bruit, *the noise*

la cathédrale, *the cathedral*
l'éducation, *f. the education*
le cuivre, *the copper*
le plomb, *the lead*
peuplé, *populous, inhabited*
pesant, *heavy.*

1. L'Angleterre est *plus grande* que la Hollande, mais elle est *plus petite* que l'Allemagne. 2. Quel est *le plus grand* pays de l'Europe? 3. C'est la Russie qui est *le plus grand* pays de l'Europe. 4. Quels sont *les plus hauts* monuments du monde? 5. Les pyramides d'Égypte sont *les plus hauts* monuments du monde. 6. La Belgique est *plus petite que* le Portugal, mais elle est *plus peuplée.* 7. La Cathédrale d'Anvers est une *des plus hautes* de l'Europe. 8. Quel est le métal *le plus précieux?* 9. L'argent est-il *plus pesant* que le fer? 10. Oui, l'argent est *plus pesant* que le fer, mais il n'est *pas aussi pesant* que l'or.

90.

1. (The) gold is heavier than (the) silver. 2. Are the Alps higher than the Pyrenees? 3. The Danube is longer than the Rhine, but the Volga is the longest river in Europe. 4. The silence of the night is more pleasant than the noise of the day. 5. The richest[2] man[1] is not always the happiest. 6. Francis is the most obedient and the most attentive scholar in the[2] whole[1] class. 7. Why have you not waited longer? 8. A good education is the greatest of blessings. 9. (The) silver is more precious than the copper. 10. London is the largest city in the world.

91.
IRREGULAR COMPARISON.

bon / bonne } *good;*	meilleur / meilleure } *better;*	le meilleur / la meilleure } *the best*
mauvais(e) *bad;*	pire* or plus mauvais, } *worse;*	le (la) pire* / le (la) plus mauvais(e) } *the worst*
petit(e), *little;*	moindre, *less;* plus petit(e), *smaller;*	le (la) moindre, *the least* le (la) plus petit(e), *the smallest.*

*pire *worse in a* moral *sense,*
plus mauvais „ physical „ .

la tempérance, *temperance*   le reproche, *the reproach*   l'événement, *m. the even*
la traduction, *the trans-*   le vent, *the wind*   déraciner, *to uproot*
    lation   la tempête, *the storm*   attrister, *to grieve*
le remède, *the remedy*   le moyen, *the means*   sévère, *strict*
le souvenir, *the recollection*   le roseau, *the reed*   violent, *violent*
le mensonge, *the false-*   le mal, *the evil*   conserver, *to preserve,*
    hood, lying   l'acier, *m. the steel*   *to keep.*

1. La bière anglaise est *meilleure* que la bière allemande. 2. Le vin de Bordeaux est *meilleur* que le vin de Rousillon, mais le vin de Champagne est le *meilleur.* 3. La traduction de mon cousin est *meilleure* que la mienne, mais la vôtre est *la meilleure.* 4. Qui est-ce qui a fait *le meilleur* thème? 5. C'est cet élève appliqué qui a fait *le meilleur* thème. 6. Le remède est souvent *pire* que le mal. 7. Quels sont *les pires* des ennemis? 8. Ce sont les flatteurs qui sont *les pires* des ennemis. 9. Où trouve-t-on *le meilleur* fer? 10. Dans quels pays fait-on *le meilleur* acier? 11. C'est en Angleterre qu'on fait le *meilleur* acier. 12. Je n'ai pas *le moindre* souvenir de cet événement.

92.
1. (The) English steel is better than (the) German steel. 2. The remedies are often worse than the diseases. 3. Be better, and you will be happier. 4. Charles' exercise is not worse than thine. 5. His reasons are better than yours. 6. The least reproach grieves my niece. 7. Your paper is not so good as theirs. 8. The strictest² laws¹ are not always the best. 9. (The) Temperance is the best means of preserving* (the) health. 10. John is my best friend. 11. The best pupils have done the best exercises. 12. The distance from London to Brighton is less than that** from London to Dover.

*Infinitive. **celle.

93.
FORMATION OF ADVERBS.

Adverbs may be formed from Adjectives by adding -ment
Adj. fidèle, *faithful,* *Adv.* fidèlement, *faithfully.*
If the Adjective ends in a consonant, -ment *is added to the* feminine: —

m. heureux, *f.* heureuse, *fortunate;* heureusement, *fortunately.*
m. actif, *f.* active, *active;* activement, *actively.*

Adjectives in nt *change this* nt *into* m: —
constant, *constant;* constamment, *constantly.*
patient, *patient;* patiemment, *patiently.*

COMPARISON OF ADVERBS.

The degrees of comparison of Adverbs are formed like those of Adjectives: —

pleasantly, more pleasantly, the most pleasantly.
agréablement, plus agréablement, le plus agréablement.

The following Adverbs form their degrees of comparison irregularly: —

bien, *well*   mieux, *better*   le mieux, *best*
mal, *badly*   pis ⎫ *worse*   le pis ⎫ *worst*
        plus mal ⎭   le plus mal ⎭
peu, *little*   moins, *less*   le moins, *least*
beaucoup, *much*   plus, *more*   le plus, *most.*

Obs. pis, worse *in a moral sense.* (See Exc. 91.)
plus mal, worse *in a physical sense.*

la plante, *the plant*
l'ambassadeur, *m. the ambassador*
l'ambassadrice, *f. the ambassadress*
l'accueil, *m. the reception, welcome*
tant pis, *so much the worse*
celui qui, *he who*
en effet, *in fact, indeed*
rendu, *rendered, given back*
imprimé, *printed, impressed*
égal, *equal.*

1. Ce livre est *bon*, il est très *bien* écrit. 2. Cette plante est *rare*; on trouve *rarement* cette plante. 3. Ton thème est *mauvais*, il est très *mal* écrit. Tant *pis!* 4. Le thème de cet écolier, qui est beaucoup *plus jeune* que vous, est *meilleur* que le vôtre, il est beaucoup *mieux* écrit. 5. Notre ambassadeur a été reçu *mieux* que le vôtre; il a reçu un *meilleur* accueil. Tant *mieux!* 6. J'ai très *peu* d'amis; j'ai *moins* d'amis que vous. 7. Regardez *bien* votre traduction, elle est *bien* écrite, mais *mal* rendue. 8. Vous êtes très *patiente*, mademoiselle, vous avez *patiemment* écouté.

FORMATION OF THE PLURAL.

94.

1. These flowers are rare. 2. We rarely[1] find[2] these flowers. 3. Your translation is good, it is better than this one*, in fact it (ce) is the best translation. 4. It is better written than the others. 5. This book is bad, it is badly printed; it is worse than yours, it is worse printed. 6. It (ce) is the worst of all. 7. So much the worse. 8. Does your aunt speak English[2] well[1]? 9. She speaks English very badly, she speaks worse English than her son and (her) daughter. 10. He has been very fortunate. *celle-ci.

95.

FORMATION OF THE PLURAL OF NOUNS (cont^d. from Ex. 23).

Singular.		Plural.
le beau château,	*the fine castle;*	les beaux châteaux.
le jeu nouveau,	*the new game;*	les jeux nouveaux.

Substantives ending in -**eau**, -**eu**, and Adjectives in -**eau** add **x** in the Plural. The following six Substantives also take **x**:

le bijou, *the jewel*	le genou, *the knee*
le caillou, *the pebble*	le hibou, *the owl*
le chou, *the cabbage*	le joujou, *the plaything*
le chameau, *the camel*	faux, *false*
le désert, *the desert*	fléchi, *bent*
l'enveloppe, *f. the envelope*	brun, *brown, dark*
le drapeau, *the banner, standard*	arboré, *hoisted*
le cheveu, *the hair*	rouge, *red*
allumé, *lighted*	bruyant, *noisy*
chargé, *loaded*	supporté, *endured*.

1. Avez-vous admiré les *châteaux* de Douvres? 2. Oui, ils sont très *beaux*. 3. Les *chameaux* ont supporté longtemps la soif. 4. Les *cailloux* sont plus utiles que les *bijoux*. 5. Où avez-vous acheté les *chapeaux* de vos enfants? 6. Les *jeux* de vos enfants sont trop bruyants. 7. Les Français ont arboré les *drapeaux* rouges. 8. Athalie a fléchi les *genoux* devant les faux *dieux*. 9. Nous avons deux *nouveaux* maîtres. 10. Vos *cheveux* sont bruns. 11. Qui a allumé les *feux?* 12. Voici vos *joujoux.*

96.

1. In these castles there are several beautiful pictures. 2. The camels have bent their knees to* be loaded (pl.). 3. The camels are the ships of the desert. 4. They have lighted the fires and hoisted the banners. 5. What beautiful games! 6. Your nephew's hair (pl.) is dark. 7. Your jewels are precious. 8. (The) jewels are not so useful as (the) pebbles. 9. These playthings are amusing. 10. Our two new masters are very strict. 11. Her hair is (are) red. 12. Mine is (are) dark. *pour.

FORMATION OF THE PLURAL.

97.

Singular.	Plural.
le cheval, *the horse*	les chevaux, *the horses*
le mal, *the evil*	les maux, *the evils*
le travail, *the work*	les travaux, *the works*
le corail, *the coral*	les coraux, *the corals*
général, *(adj.) general*	généraux, *general.*

Most Nouns in -al, *and a few in* -ail, *change this ending into* -aux *in the Plural.*

(For Exceptions see Eugène's Comp. French Gr. §§ 19-21.)

la patience, *patience*
le journal, *the newspaper*
tout, *m.* (*pl.* tous) ⎫
toute, *f.* (*pl.* toutes) ⎭ *the whole, all, every*
l'écaille, *f. the scale (of fish etc.)*
l'amiral, *the admiral*
avantageux, *profitable*
nourri, *fed, nourished*
souffert, *suffered*
la laine, *the wool.*

1. Les *chevaux* sont [des] *animaux* très utiles. 2. Y a-t-il des *canaux* dans ces pays? 3. Quand aurez-vous fini vos *travaux?* 4. Quels sont les *métaux* les plus utiles? 5. Vos *neveux* ont-ils vendu leurs *chevaux?* 6. Les *amiraux* anglais ont-ils pris ces *drapeaux* sur* l'ennemi? 7. Votre père a-t-il lu les *journaux* d'aujourd'hui? 8. Les *coraux* sont rouges. 9. Ils ont souffert ces *maux* avec patience. 10. Ces *travaux* sont très avantageux au commerce. 11. Les *journaux* du soir ne sont pas arrivés. 12. Dieu a donné des plumes aux oiseaux, des écailles aux poissons et de la laine aux brebis.

* from.

98.

1. The canals are profitable for (the) commerce. 2. (The) men are equal before God. 3. Have you read the evening papers*? 4. No, but I have read the morning papers*. 5. (The) English[2] horses[1] are better than (the) French[2] horses[1], they are better fed. 6. (The) iron is the most useful of all (the) metals. 7. These birds are very fine. 8. There are many animals in this forest. 9. Have they finished their works? 10. No, they have not yet finished their works. 11. Spain is nearly as large as France. 12. The port of Marseilles is the largest port in (of) France.

* papers of the evening, morning.

99.
PLURAL OF NOUNS (Irregular).

le ciel, *the sky, heaven*   les cieux, *skies, the heavens*
l'œil, *the eye*   les yeux, *the eyes*
l'aïeul, *the grandfather*   { les aïeux, *the ancestors*
                           { les aïeuls, *the grandfathers.*

Obs. ciel and œil also form their plural regularly (see *Eugène's Comp. Gram.* § 21).

raconter, *to relate, to tell*
la neige, *the snow*
la gloire, *the glory*
le grain, *the grain, seed*
la moutarde, *the mustard*
l'action, *f. the action*
l'oreille, *f. the ear*
la bouche, *the mouth*

la vertu, *virtue*
bleu (*plur.* bleus) *blue*
levé, *lifted, raised*
simple, *plain, simple*
semblable, *similar, like*
mal aux yeux, *sore eyes*
comme, *as*
tout ce qu'il faut, *all that is required.*

1. Les *cieux* racontent la gloire de Dieu. 2. Vos *aïeuls* parlent toujours de la gloire de leurs *aïeux*. 3. Votre neveu a mal aux *yeux*. 4. Les cheveux de mes *aïeuls* sont blancs comme la neige. 5. Les malheureux ont levé les *yeux* au ciel. 6. Le royaume des *cieux* est semblable à un grain de moutarde. 7. Les *généraux* ont perdu deux batailles. 8. L'or n'est pas le plus utile de tous les *métaux*.

100.

1. Our ancestors were more simple than we. 2. (The) Italy is under one of the finest skies of Europe. 3. His eyes are blue. 4. We have honoured the virtues of our ancestors by our actions. 5. Have you still your two grandfathers? 6. (The) gold is more precious than all the other metals. 7. (The) man has two eyes, two ears and one mouth. 8. The English admirals have captured three Spanish vessels. 9. Our grandfather has sore eyes.

101.
THE PARTITIVE GENITIVE (compare Ex. 49).

le pain, *the bread*   du pain, *some or any bread*
la viande, *the meat*   de la viande, - - *meat*
l'eau, *the water*   de l'eau - - *water*
l'herbe, *the grass*   de l'herbe - - *grass*
les livres, *the books*   des livres, - - *books*
les amis, *the friends*   des amis, - - *friends*
les poires, *the pears.*   des poires, - - *pears.*

THE PARTITIVE GENITIVE.

Obs. *Bear in mind that in English* some *or* any *are often not expressed, but simply understood. Translate for practice:* —

the butter, some (or any) butter, of the butter, to the butter, butter;
the beer, some (or any) beer, of the beer, to the beer, beer;
the ink, some (or any) ink, of the ink, to the ink, ink;
the horses, some (or any) horses, of the horses, to the horses, horses;
some evils, the evils, evils; gold, the gold, any gold;
the shame, any shame, to the shame; the heroes, of the heroes,
to the heroes, any heroes; the silver, of the silver, some silver.

la soie, *the silk*
la mine, *the mine*
la houille, *the coals*
la toile, *the linen*
la salade, *the salad*
la vache, *the cow*
l'huile, *f. the oil*
le vinaigre, *the vinegar*
le bétail,* *the cattle*
l'étain, *m. the tin*
le cuivre, *the copper*
la laitue, *the lettuce*
*pl. les bestiaux.

le lait, *the milk*
le café, *the coffee*
le café à la crème, *coffee and cream*
le sucre, *the sugar*
le petit pain, *the roll*
le poivre, *the pepper*
le sel, *the salt*
enfin, *at last, in short*
le chocolat, *the chocolate*
le bonbon, *the sweetmeat*
les soieries, *the silk-stuffs*
il fait, *he makes*

le papier à lettres, *the letter-paper*
le timbre-poste, *postage-stamp*
exporter, *to export*
on y va, *coming!*
que désirez-vous? *what will you have?*
moi, *me, I*
s'il vous plaît, *if you please*
il me faut, *I want*
la gomme élastique, *the india-rubber.*

1. L'Italie exporte *de la* soie, *de l'*huile et *des* fruits. 2. On trouve dans les mines de l'Angleterre *du* fer, *de la* houille, *de l'*étain, *du* cuivre et beaucoup *d'*autres métaux. 3. L'Irlande exporte *de la* toile, *du* beurre et *des* œufs (*f.* silent). 4. Garçon! 5. On y va, monsieur! 6. Que désirez-vous, monsieur? 7. Apportez-moi *du* café à la crème, *du* sucre, *du* beurre et *des* petits pains. 8. Apportez-moi aussi *du* sel, *du* poivre, *de la* moutarde, *de l'*huile, *du* vinaigre, *des* laitues, *des* œufs, enfin, tout ce qu'il faut pour faire *de la* salade. 9. Papa, donnez-moi, s'il vous plaît, *de l'*argent. 10. Pourquoi *de l'*argent? 11. Pour acheter *des* bonbons et *des* joujoux. 12. Il me faut *de l'*encre, *des* plumes, *du* papier à lettres, *des* enveloppes et *des* timbres-poste.

102.

1. Switzerland exports cheese, butter, cattle, silk-stuffs and watches. 2. Give me, if you please, some milk. 3. Do you want wine or beer? 4. I want some water. 5. Have you any friends? 6. Have they given grass to the cows? 7. Has the servant bought any eggs? 8. The shoemaker makes shoes and boots. 9. Will you have tea or coffee? 10. I want some chocolate and eggs. 11. There is iron, lead, copper, and tin in the mines of England. 12. (The) silver is heavier than (the) copper.

103.

beaucoup de vin, *much* wine;*
peu de viande, *little meat;*
plus d'argent, *more money;*
moins d'huile, *less oil;*
trop de sel, *too much salt;*
combien d'eau, *how much water;*
autant de fruit, *as much fruit;*
pas tant (autant) de sucre, *not so much sugar;*
pas de poivre, *no (not any) pepper;*
point d'argent, *no money (at all);*
assez de thé, *enough tea;*

beaucoup de livres, *many* books*
peu de pommes, *few apples*
plus d'amis, *more friends*
moins d'hommes, *fewer men*
trop de frais, *too many expenses*
combien de francs, *how many francs*
autant de poires, *as many pears*
pas tant (autant) de noix, *not so many nuts*
pas de cerises, *no (not any) cherries*
point de Suisses, *no Switzers*
assez de lettres, *enough lettres.*

* *Observe the difference between* **Singular** *and* **Plural** *in English.*

Adverbs of **quantity** *and* **negation** *take simply* de (*and not* du, de l', de la, des). *Except* bien (*in the sense of* beaucoup, *much, many*) *which takes the* **Partitive** *article.*

bien du bruit, *much noise,*
bien des hommes, *many men,*
le raisin, *the grapes*
une grappe de raisin, *a bunch of grapes*
un grain de raisin, *a grape*

but

beaucoup de bruit
beaucoup d'hommes.
des raisins secs, *raisins*
l'étranger, *the stranger, foreigner*
produit, *produces*
le blé, *the corn.*

Obs. *Than and as after adverbs of comparison are translated by* que.

1. La France produit-elle *du* vin et *du* blé? 2. La France produit *beaucoup de* vin et *de* blé. 3. Désirez-vous *des* pommes? 4. *Combien de* pommes désirez-vous? 5. Je désire deux pommes. 6. Je désire *autant de* pommes que mon frère. 7. Avez-vous *du* pain, *de l'*eau, *de la* viande et *des* poires? 8. Nous avons *assez de* pain, *d'*eau, *de* viande et *de* poires. 9. Ont-ils *du* vinaigre, *de l'*huile, *de la* moutarde, et *des* petits pains? 10. Non, monsieur, ils n'ont *pas de* vinaigre, *d'*huile, *de* moutarde et *de* petits pains. 11. Avez-vous *de* l'argent sur vous? 12. Non, mon ami, je n'ai *point d'*argent. 13. La Belgique exporte *moins de* houille que l'Angleterre. 14. N'y a-t-il pas *trop de* sel dans la soupe?

104.

1. There are many foreigners in (à) Paris. 2. How many inhabitants are there in London? 3. There are more inhabitants in London than in (the) Switzerland. 4. This scholar has no mistakes in his exercise. 5. They have less money than the banker, but they have also fewer cares than the banker. 6. You have given too much wine to his child. 7. Have you bought grapes or raisins? 8. I have bought grapes, but I have not bought any raisins. 9. This poor woman has many children but little money. 10. Do you want some wine, sir? 11. No, I have had too much wine.

ADVERBS OF QUANTITY. 55

105.

une tasse de thé,	*a cup of tea*
une douzaine de crayons,	*a dozen of pencils*
un verre d'eau,	*a glass of water*
une corbeille de cerises,	*a basket of cherries*
une livre d'huile,	*a pound of oil*
une livre de raisins secs,	*a pound of raisins.*

After Substantives denoting quantity *or* capacity, *the* Partitive *Genitive is (as after Adverbs of quantity) expressed by* de, *(and* not *by* du, de la, de l', des*).*

Obs. *Similarly only* de *is used before a Substantive taken in a partitive sense, if preceded by an* Adjective: *as,*

du vin, *some wine*, de bon vin, *some good wine*
de la salade, *some salad*, d'excellente salade, *excellent salad*
des amis, *friends*, de vrais amis, *true friends*.

le jambon, *the ham* la bagatelle, *the trifle*
la saucisse, *the sausage* l'aune, *f. the ell*
la terre, *the earth, the estate* la couverture, *the cover, the blanket*
le produit, *the product* la carafe, *the decanter*
l'espèce, *f. the kind* la plume métallique, *the steel pen*
la foule, *the crowd, great quantity* le morceau, *the piece, morsel, bit*
le poisson, *the fish* la tranche, *the slice*
la plupart (de), *most* la cave, *the cellar.*

1. Désirez-vous *du* jambon ou *de la* saucisse? 2. Donnez-moi une tranche *de* jambon, s'il vous plaît. 3. Voici un *verre de* vin et une bouteille *de* bière. 4. La terre que nous avons en France est riche en produits *de* toute espèce; il y a *de* très bons vins, *d'*excellents fruits, *de* grandes forêts où il y a beaucoup *de* gibier, *de* petites rivières, et *des* lacs où il y a une foule *de* poissons. 5. Voilà bien *du* bruit pour une bagatelle. 6. Nous avons acheté vingt et une aunes *de* toile et une paire *de* couvertures. 7. Garçon, une tasse *de* café à la crème!

106.

1. Why have you not given a piece of bread to this child? 2. He does not want bread, he wants money. 3. How many pounds of grapes have you bought (fem. plur.)? 4. I have not bought any grapes. 5. There are fewer mountains in Holland than in Switzerland, but there are more canals in Holland. 6. Bring me a glass of wine and a slice of ham, if you please. 7. We have good wine in the cellar. 8. Here are excellent pears and fine nuts. 9. There are very large cities in England. 10. Here is a cup of coffee and a glass of water.

ADJECTIVES WITH THREE TERMINATIONS.

107.
ADJECTIVES WITH THREE TERMINATIONS.

Masculine.		Feminine.	
before a Cons.;	bef. a vowel or sil. h.;		
beau	bel,	belle,	*fine, beautiful*
fou	fol,	folle,	*foolish*
mou	mol,	molle,	*soft*
nouveau	nouvel,	nouvelle,	*new*
vieux	vieil,	vieille,	*old.*

le gendarme, *the policeman*
la cire, *the wax*
le volume, *the volume*
différent, *different*
auparavant *(adv.)* ⎫
avant, *(prep.)* ⎭ *before*
à la mode, *in fashion, fashionable*
l'ivrogne', m. *the drunkard*
l'hôpital m. *the hospital*
à droite et à gauche, *right and left*
souhaiter, *to wish*
laid, *ugly*

porté, *worn, borne, carried*
l'avenir, m. *the future*
à l'avenir, *for the future*
la nouvelle, *the news*
avoir des nouvelles de, *to hear from*
tous les jours, *every day*
tout le jour, *the whole day*
toujours, *always*
l'orage, m. *the thunderstorm*
l'abricot, m. *the apricot*
surpris, *surprised, overtaken*
quel! *what (a) .. !*

1. Où as-tu acheté ce *beau* chien et ce *bel* oiseau? 2. Chez la *belle* jardinière. 3. Et ce *bel* habit? — Chez le *vieux* tailleur. 4. Ce *nouveau* volume des œuvres de Walter Scott est très-intéressant. 5. Un *nouvel* habit est un habit différent de celui qu'on avait auparavant. 6. Un habit *neuf* est un habit qui n'a pas encore été porté. 7. Un habit *nouveau* est un habit à la mode. 8. Cette poire est *molle*. 9. Quel *bel* enfant! 10. Oui, il est très *beau*. 11. Quels *beaux* enfants! 12. Mais non, ils ne sont pas *beaux*, ils sont très laids. 13. Ce *vieux* soldat et ce *vieil* ivrogne sont maintenant à l'hôpital. 14. La ville de Chester est très ancienne. 15. Ce gendarme est un ancien soldat.

108.

1. He (has) put on a new coat every day. 2. This new fashioned coat is very expensive. 3. Henry has been surprised by a storm, he has put on another coat. 4. What [a] fine apricot! 5. What fine apricots! 6. I wish (to) my brother a happy new year. 7. These two gentleman are old friends. 8. This old man is a retired soldier. 9. Has your cousin heard from his father? 10. The city of Marseilles is very old; it is the oldest[2] city[1] in France. 11. This wax is very soft. 12. Have they heard from their old aunt? 13. Yes, they have heard from their old aunt; she has a new servant. 14. What a beautiful new hat you have there!

ADJECTIVES.

109.

Adjectives which form their feminine irregularly.

doux,	douce,	*sweet, soft*	sec,	sèche,	*dry*
faux,	fausse,	*false*	frais,	fraîche,	*fresh*
blanc,	blanche,	*white*	bénin,	bénigne,	*benignant*
franc,	franche,	*frank, candid*	malin,	maligne,	*malignant*
public,	publique,	*public*	long,	longue,	*long*
grec,	grecque,	*Greek*	favori,	favorite,	*favourite.*

(Compare Eugène's French Gram. § 29, 34, 35 for an explanation of these seeming irregularities.)

la vanité, *vanity*
la modestie, *modesty*
le linge blanc, *clean linen*
la fraise, *the strawberry*
la groseille, *the currant*
la groseille à maquereau, *the gooseberry*
la chemise, *the shirt*
la couleur, *the colour*
la crevette, *the shrimp*

la blanchisseuse, *the laundress*
le miel, *the honey*
boire, *to drink*
n'est-ce pas? { *is it? is it not? are they? are they not? have they? &c.*
une demi livre, *half a pound*
une livre et demie, *a pound and a half*
nu-pieds, } *barefoot*
pieds-nus, }

Obs. demi and nu are invariable before the Substantive, but variable after it:—

1. Ma poire est plus *douce* que ta pomme. 2. Le bleu est ma couleur *favorite*. 3. Cette bière est encore très *fraîche*, elle n'est pas *bonne* à boire. 4. Votre traduction est *longue*, n'est-ce pas? 5. Une *franche* vanité déplaît moins qu'une *fausse* modestie. 6. La neige est *blanche*. 7. La blanchisseuse a-t-elle apporté le linge *blanc*? 8. Cette nouvelle n'est-elle pas *fausse*? 9. Apportez-moi, s'il vous plaît, un verre d'eau *fraîche*. 10. Les fraises sont plus *douces* que les groseilles. 11. Vos chemises ne sont pas encore *sèches*. 12. Ma traduction *grecque* est très *longue*.

110.

1. Here is a pretty rose, it is your favourite flower, is it not? 2. The way from here to London is very long. 3. Your clean linen is not yet dry. 4. This fish is fresh, but these shrimps are not fresh. 5. I have not yet seen your new house. 6. Have you any sweet[2] pears[1] to sell? 7. Yes, and I have also excellent raisins. 8. How (much) do you sell the pears? 9. One franc a[*] dozen and the raisins 90 cents a[*] pound. 10. Well, give me two dozens of pears and half a pound of raisins. 11. Have you any grapes? Yes sir! 12. Bring me a glass of fresh[2] water[1], if you please. *the.

111.
FIRST CONJUGATION.

Future.	Conditional.
Je parlerai, *I shall speak*	Je parlerais, *I should speak*
tu parleras, *thou wilt speak*	tu parlerais, *thou wouldst speak*
il (elle) parlera, *he will speak*	il (elle) parlerait, *he would speak*
nous parlerons, *we shall speak*	nous parlerions, *we should speak*
vous parlerez, *you will speak*	vous parleriez, *you would speak*
(ils)elles parleront, *they will speak.*	ils(elles) parleraient, *they would „*
parlerai-je? etc. *Shall I speak,*	parlerais-je? etc. *Should I speak,*
je ne parlerai pas, etc.	je ne parlerais pas, etc.
ne parlerai-je pas? etc.	ne parlerais-je pas? etc.

Like parler *conjugate:* — accompagner, *to accompany;* rester, *to stay.*

le bateau à vapeur, *the steamboat*
le cap de la Bonne Espérance, *the Cape of Good Hope*
le débarcadère, *the landing-place*

rentrer, *to go in again, to return home*
abandonner, *abandon*
comme il faut, *properly, gentlemanly*
obstiné, *obstinate.*

Practice: j'accompagnerai mon frère lundi prochain, etc.
accompagneras-tu ton cousin demain? etc.
je travaillerais ce soir, si je n'étais pas malade, etc.

1. A qui *apporterez*-vous ces fraises? 2. J'*apporterai* ces fraises à notre vieille voisine. 3. *Accompagnera*-t-elle sa tante à Berlin? 4. *Parleras*-tu à ton oncle? 5. Vous *porterez* cette lettre à la poste. 6. Quand elles *rentreront*, je serai sorti. 7. Le train *arrivera* à cinq heures. 8. Les bateaux à vapeur du cap de la Bonne Espérance *arriveront* jeudi prochain, le quinze août. 9. *Travailleront*-elles ce soir? 10. Je *récompenserais* ce garçon, s'il méritait une récompense. 11. Le maître *récompenserait* les élèves, s'ils avaient travaillé comme il faut. 12. Qui n'*aimerait* pas ses parents? 13. Elles *abandonneraient* leur projet, si elles n'étaient pas si obstinées.

112.

1. I shall not abandon this child. 2. Will he give any money to the old laundress? 3. Two trains will arrive at half-past eleven. 4. Will you think of your duties? 5. I should inhabit this house, if I had enough money. 6. When you (will) return, you will find the house shut. 7. We shall accompany our mother to the railway station. 8. We should also accompany our cousin to the pier, if we had (the) time. 9. These studious young ladies will work the whole evening. 10. My old neighbours would not work, if they were tired. 11. Would you reward the pupils, if they had not deserved a recompense? 12. He would study, if he were not so idle.

113.

Compound Tenses (with avoir).

Learn the Compound Tenses (Indicative Mood) of **aimer** *(see pp. 96—97).*

le souper, *the supper* souper, *to sup*
le facteur, *the postman* demander, *to ask, to beg, to order*
la dépêche, *the dispatch, message* banni, *banished*
jusqu'à, *until, as far as* assidûment, *assiduously*

Practice: J'ai parlé de la guerre, etc. Aussitôt que j'eus fini, etc.
N'avais-je pas trouvé des noix? etc. Quand j'aurai travaillé, etc.

1. J'ai *mangé* assez de cerises. 2. Il *a travaillé* assez longtemps. 3. Mes amis *n'ont*-ils *pas* voyagé depuis trois semaines? 4. Pourquoi le maître *n'a-t-il pas puni* ces élèves paresseux? 5. Parce qu'ils *ont promis* de travailler assidûment à l'avenir. 6. Dès que j'*eus dîné*, je quittai la maison. 7. *Avez*-vous *demandé* à Monsieur Jacques si sa sœur arrivera ce soir? 8. Nous *avions* déjà *soupé* quand vous *êtes arrivé*. 9. Nous *aurons* déjà *quitté* Bordeaux quand vous arriverez. 10. Les garçons *auront apporté* du vin et de l'eau. 11. Ils *auraient* aussi *apporté* de la bière, si elle était bonne à boire. 12. Aussitôt que vous *eûtes envoyé* votre dépêche, le facteur apporta une lettre. 13. Les Grecs *ont* souvent *banni* leurs grands hommes. 14. Nous aurions visité le palais, s'il avait été ouvert.

114.

In this Exercise render the English **Imperfect** *by the French* **Past Indefinite:** —

1. Did you speak? 2. No, I did not speak. 3. Did he see my father? 4. No, but he saw your mother. 5. What did they bring? 6. They brought a fish. 7. Did you play this morning? 8. Did he accompany his sister? 9. Yes, he accompanied his sister as far as Bedford. 10. We sold our house.

---

11. You had already finished your exercise, when we came (are come). 12. If they had worked, they would have finished their book. 13. We should have brought our books, if we had met our master. 14. He would have worked longer, if it had not been too late. 15. I should have left this country long ago, if I had not so many friends.

115.
Personal Pronouns (Pronoms Personnels).
Singular.

	First Pers.	Second Pers.	Third Pers.
Subj. or *Nom.*	je, *I*	tu, *thou*	il, elle, *he, she, it*
Dir. Obj. or *Acc.*	me, *me*	te, *thee*	le, la, *him, her, it*
Ind. Obj. or *Dat.*	me, *to me*	te, *to thee*	lui (m. & f.) (y) *to him, to her, to it.*

Plural.

Nom.	nous, *we*	vous, *you*	ils, elles, *they*
Acc.	nous, *us*	vous, *you*	les (m. & f.) *them*
Dat.	nous, *to us*	vous, *to you*	leur (m. & f.) y, *to them.*

Accusative:

Charles me* loue,	*Charles praises* me
„ te* trompe,	„ *deceives* thee
„ le*, la* blâme,	„ *blames* him, her
„ nous quitte,	„ *leaves* us
„ vous aime,	„ *loves* you
„ les(m.&f.) loue,	„ *praises* them

Dative:

Jean me* parle,	*John speaks* to me
„ te* donne,	„ *gives* to thee
„ lui (m.&f.) donne,	„ „ to him, her
„ nous répond,	„ *replies* to us
„ vous prête,	„ *lends* to you
„ leur donne,	„ *gives* to them.

*Before a verb beginning with a vowel m', t', l': as
il m'aime, il t'aime; il l'aime (him or her).

Practice: — Acc. { Alfred me trouva, etc.
{ Mon ami m'abandonna.
Dat. { elle me montra le chemin, etc.
{ il m'ordonne de rester, etc.

le filou, *the pickpocket*
l'injustice, *f. the injustice, wrong*
déranger, *to disturb, to put out of*
confier, *to confide, entrust [order*
blâmer, *to blame*
tromper, *to deceive*
prêter, *to lend*
conseiller (à), *to advise*
pardonner (à), *to forgive*
répliquer, *to answer, to reply.*

Obs. Demander, *to ask for*, takes a **dative** of the person, and an **accusative** of the thing: as,
Il lui a demandé son nom. *He asked him for his name.*

1. Vous *me* dérangez. 2. Je *te* regarde. 3. Il *le* loue et elle *la* blâme. 4. Je *le* donne à votre père. 5. Je *te* donne l'argent. 6. Tu *me* donneras ces livres. 7. Elle *lui* confie son argent. 8. Vouz *m'*avez trompé. 9. Ces filous *te* tromperont. 10. Est-ce que vous aimez ces enfants? 11. Oui, je *les* aime. 12. Vos sœurs *nous* ont écrit samedi dernier. 13. Vous *m'*oubliez. 14. Ayez la bonté de *nous* prêter votre livre. 15. Votre frère m'a écrit, je *lui* répondrai demain.

Parse all the Personal Pronouns in the Exercise above.

116.

1. You will forgive me. 2. I lend you this book. 3. He gave thee money. 4. You deceive him. 5. We were looking for you. 6. We were listening [to] you. 7. You shall reply to them (to him) this evening. 8. We find them. 9. I advised (to) him to stay. 10. She praises you much. 11. You will soon* forget¹ me. 12. We bring you (a) good news. 13. He forgave us all our wrongs. 14. Do you like (the) ham? 15. Yes, I like it much. 16. Look [for] your niece, you will find her in the garden.

117.
PERSONAL PRONOUNS (continued).

Accusative.

Me loue-t-il?	or Est-ce qu'il me loue?	Does he praise	me?
Te trompe-t-il?	,,	te trompe?	,, deceive	thee?
Le, la blâme-t-il?	,,	le, la blâme?	,, blame	him, her?
Nous aime-t-il?	,,	nous aime?	,, love	us?
Vous honore-t-il?	,,	vous honore?	,, honour	you?
Les (m.&f.) trouve-t-il?	,,	les trouve?	,, find	them?

Dative.

Me (te) parle-t-il? or Est-ce qu'il me (te) parle? Does he speak to me, to thee?
Lui (m.& f.) ,, ? ,, lui ,, ? ,, to him, to her?
Nous (vous) ,, ? ,, nous, (vous) ,, ? ,, to us, to you?
Leur (m.&f.) ,, ? ,, leur ,, ? ,, to them?

Negative and Interrogative.

Ne me (te, le, etc.) frappe-t-il pas? } Does he not strike me, thee,
or Est-ce qu'il ne me (te, etc.) frappe pas? } him? etc.

l'inspecteur, the inspector
négligent, careless
l'aiguille, f. the needle
l'épingle, f. the pin
taquiner, to tease
cependant, yet, meanwhile
se donner de la peine, to take trouble.

admirer, to admire
examiner, to examine
récompenser, to reward
approuver, to approve
imiter, to imitate
crier, to cry.

1. Admirez-vous notre théâtre? 2. *L'*admirez-vous? 3. Oui, nous *l'*admirons, mais nous *ne le* visiterons *pas*. 4. Est-ce qu'il étudie sa leçon? 5. Est-ce qu'il *l'*étudie? 6. Non, il *ne l'*étudie *pas* à présent, mais il *l'*étudiera ce soir. 7. Pourquoi *ne les* cherchent-ils *pas?* 8. Ils *ne la* quitteront *pas*. 9. *Vous* aime-t-elle? (Est-ce qu'elle *vous* aime?) 10. Non, elle *ne nous* aime *pas*. 11. Pourquoi *ne vous* aime-t-elle *pas?* (Pourquoi est-ce qu'elle *ne vous* aime *pas?*) 12. Parce que nous *la* taquinons toujours. 13. *M'*aimez-vous? (Est-ce que vous *m'*aimez?) 14. *Lui* montrerez vous ce livre? (Est-ce que vous *lui*, etc.)? 15. Oui, je *lui* montrerai ce livre, mais je *ne lui* donnerai *pas* ce livre.

Un voleur[1] entra une nuit par la fenêtre dans la chambre d'un pauvre homme, et se mit[2] à tâtonner[3] à droite et à gauche. „Mon ami," lui crie celui-ci, qui ne dormait[4] pas, ne vous donnez pas la peine de chercher plus longtemps; vous ne sauriez[5] rien trouver, pendant la nuit, dans un lieu[6] où je ne trouve rien pendant le jour.

1) thief; 2) began; 3) feel; 4) slept; 5) can; 6) place.

118.

All interrogative sentences to be translated both *ways*.

1. Will the inspector examine the pupil? 2. Yes, he will examine him; but he will not reward him. 3. Do they admire her? 4. Yes, they admire her much, yet they do not love her. 5. Why do they not love her? 6. Because she does not love them. 7. Do your cousins approve [of] your conduct? 8. Yes, they approve [of] it, yet they do not imitate it. 9. Why do they not imitate it? 10. Because they are too careless. 11. Will you shut the door? 12. Yes, I shall shut it. 13. Would you give (to) him the book? 14. Would you give (to) her the needles and pins? 15. Will you show (to) us the pictures? 16. Yes, we shall show you the pictures; we shall also show them to your friends.

119.
PERSONAL PRONOUNS (continued).
Accusative.

Il m' (t', l') a récompensé.	*He has rewarded* me, (thee, him).
Il l' (f.) a récompensée.	„ her.
Il nous (vous, les) a récompensés.	„ us, (you, them [m]).
Il les (f.) a récompensées.	„ them (f.)

Dative.

Il m' (t') a parlé.	*He has spoken* to me (to thee).
Il lui (m. & f.) a parlé.	„ to him, to her.
Il nous (vous) a parlé.	„ to us, (to you).
Il leur (m. & f.) a parlé.	„ to them.

Has he left me? etc.
M'a-t-il quitté?
Nous a-t-il quittés? etc. *or* Est-ce qu'il m'a quitté?
„ nous a quittés? etc.

He has not struck me (us), etc.
Il *ne* m'a *pas* frappé.
Il *ne* nous a *pas* frappés, etc.

Has he not struck me, (us)? etc.
Ne m'a-t-il *pas* frappé?
Ne nous a-t-il *pas* frappés? etc. *or* Est-ce qu'il *ne* t'a *pas* frappé?
„ *ne* nous a *pas* frappés?

The **Past Participle** *conjugated with* **avoir** *agrees in* **Gender** *and* **Number** *with the* **Object** *(Accusative only) when that* **Object** *stands* **before** *the Past Participle in the sentence:—*

No agreement.	Agreement.
J'ai récompensé cette fille.	Voici la fille que j'ai récompensée; Je l'ai récompensée.
J'ai récompensé ces garçons.	Voici les garçons que j'ai récompensés; Je les ai récompensés;
J'ai récompensé ces filles.	Voici les filles que j'ai récompensées; Je les ai récompensées.

(*See also the Paradigms above, and the Eugène's French Gram.* §§ 160—164.)

la bibliothèque, *the library*
le bibliothécaire, *the librarian*
la librairie, *the bookseller's shop or business*
le libraire, *the bookseller*

l'estampe, *f. the engraving, print*
la boîte, *the box*
plusieurs fois, *several times*
ressembler à, *to resemble, to be like*
obéi à, *obeyed.*

1. Je *ne vous* ai *pas* encore montré ma bibliothèque. 2. Je *vous* aurais déjà montré mes livres, si j'avais eu le temps. 3. Où est votre cousin? 4. Il est chez le libraire. 5. *Lui* avez-vous dit que mon oncle d'Amérique *l'*a invité à souper? 6. Je *ne lui* ai *pas* dit cela, je *ne lui* ai *pas* parlé. 7. Ces estampes sont très belles, de qui *les* avez-vous (de qui est-ce que vous *les* avez) reçues? 8. Je *ne les* ai *pas* reçues, mon cousin *les* a prêtées à mon frère. 9. *Ne leur* as-tu *pas* rendu les cahiers qu'ils *t'*avaient prêtés? 10. Ce filou *ne vous* a-t-il *pas* trompés plusieurs fois? 11. Non, monsieur, il *ne nous* a *pas* trompés. 12. *Vous* a-t-elle recommandées? 13. Oui, madame, elle *nous* a recommandées à sa cousine. 14. Nous *vous* avons obéi avec plaisir. 15. Elle *lui* ressemble.

Un certain comte était connu[1] pour un mauvais débiteur[2] qui amusait ses créanciers[3] par de vaines[4] promesses. Un de ses amis prit[5] occasion de lui dire[6]: „Vraiment, c'est bien dommage[7] que la fortune néglige[8] un homme qui promet[9] tant."

1) known; 2) debtor; 3) creditors; 4) vain, idle; 5) took; 6) to say; 7) great pity; 8) should neglect; 9) promises.

120.

1. Have you found my English grammar? 2. Yes, I (have) found it in the garden. 3. Have you shown (to) them your fine garden? 4. I should have shown them our garden, if they had visited us. 5. Have you accompanied her? 6. No, I have not accompanied her. 7. Has the waiter brought that bottle of wine which you have ordered? 8. No, he has not yet brought it. 9. Where did you buy (Indef.) these beautiful books? 10. I did not buy (Indef.) them, I received them from my aunt. 11. She also gave (Indef.) me a box of steel-pens.

12. Will not your friends forget you? 13. They have already forgotten us. 14. We have praised him. 15. We have obeyed him (dat.). 16. Did you obey her (dat.)? 17. Did you see (Indef.) them? 18. Do you resemble them (dat.)? 19. Did you speak (Indef.) to them? 20. Have you spoken to them? 21. No, we have not spoken to them.

121.
PERSONAL PRONOUNS (continued).

En, *of it, of them, with them; some, any* (expressed or understood).

Avez-vous de l'argent?	*Have you any money?*
Oui, j'en ai. Non, je n'en ai point.	*Yes, I have* (some). *No I have not* any.
Désirez-vous des pommes?	*Do you want apples?*
Oui, j'en désire.	*Yes, I do (want* some).
Non, je n'en désire point.	*No, I do not want* any.
A-t-il une plume?	*Has he a pen?*
Oui, il en a une; il en a plusieurs.	*Yes, he has* one; *he has several.*
Doutez-vous de sa fidélité?	*Do you doubt (of) his fidelity?*
Oui, j'en doute.	*Yes, I do (doubt* of it).
Non, je n'en doute pas.	*No, I do not (doubt* of it).
Êtes-vous content de sa conduite?	*Are you satisfied with his conduct?*
Oui, j'en suis content.	*Yes, I am (satisfied* with it).
Non, je n'en suis pas content.	*No I am not satisfied* with it.

(*See also Eugène's French Gram.* §§ 50, 193—195.)

Practice: J'en ai, tu en as, etc.   En aurais-je? etc.
Je n'en avais pas, etc.   N'en aurais-je pas? etc.

le besoin, *the want, need*
avoir besoin de, *to want, to be in need of*
la paire, *the pair*
fâché (de), *sorry for*
fâché (contre), *angry (with)*
car, *(conj.) for*
pour, *(prep.) for*
au lieu de, *instead of*
emprunter, *to borrow*
le buffet, *the sideboard, refreshment-[room.*

1. Si vous avez besoin d'argent, je vous *en* donnerai.
2. Oui, j'*en* ai besoin. 3. Avez-vous des poires? 4. Oui, j'*en* ai encore six douzaines. 5. Et des abricots? 6. Non, je n'*en* ai plus; je les ai tous vendus. Tant pis! 7. Y a-t-il encore de l'encre dans l'encrier? 8. Oui, il y *en* a encore, mais bientôt il n'y *en* aura plus. 9. Combien de lettres avez-vous reçues? 10. J'*en* ai reçu trois ce soir, mais je n'*en* ai pas reçu ce matin. 11. Où sont mes bottes? 12. Elles sont chez le cordonnier. 13. Tant pis, car je n'*en* ai qu'une paire.

122.

1. Has the gardener any fruit? 2. Yes, he has (some). 3. Are there chairs enough in this room? 4. Yes, there are (enough of them). 5. Do you want any ham? 6. No, I don't want any now, but I shall eat some

this evening. 7. Will the Jew give you a thousand francs for* your horse? 8. No, he will not give me so much for* it 9. I have two grammars, how many (of them) have you? 10. I have three, but my brother has not any. 11. We shall borrow some money, we are in need of some, for we have [none left] (no more of it). 12. We have lessons to learn this evening; have you also (of them)? 13. How many children has she? — Seven. *of.

123.

PERSONAL PRONOUNS (continued).

Y, *to it, at it, in it; to them, at them, in them; there, thither* (expressed or understood).

Consentirez-vous à ma proposition?	*Shall you consent to my proposal?*
J'y consentirai, mais mon frère n'y consentira pas.	*I shall consent to it, but my brother will not consent to it.*
Contribuera-t-il à ces frais?	*Will he contribute to these expenses?*
Y contribuera-t-il?	*Will he contribute to them?*
Il y contribuera;	*He will contribute to them;*
mais nous n'y contribuerons pas.	*but we shall not contribute to them.*
Avez-vous été à Londres?	*Have you been in London?*
Y avez vous été? Nous y avons été.	*Have you been there? We have b. there.*
Je n'y ai pas été cette année,	*I have not been there this year,*
mais j'y fus pendant l'Exposition,	*but I was there during the Exhibition.*
et j'y retournerai l'année prochaine.	*and I shall return there next year.*

(*See also Eugène's French Gram.* §§ 50, 194, 195.)

124.

le billet, *the ticket, note*
le bureau, *the desk, the office*
il y a une heure, *an hour ago*
hier au soir, *yesternight*

le pupitre, *the desk*
regarder, *to look, to concern*
penser à } *to think of, to consider.*
songer à }

1. Have your sisters been to the concert to-day? 2. No, they have not been there to-day, but they have been there yesternight. 3. If they have no tickets, I will give them some. 4. Have you considered your proposal? 5. I am considering it now. 6. Have the pupils been to church? 7. Yes, they have (been there); they will return there this evening. 8. If you are in want of paper, my father will give you some. 9. Is he in (at) the office? 10. He was there an hour ago, but if he is not there now, you will find some on his desk. 11. Are you speaking of our festivities? 12. Yes, we are (speaking of them). 13. Are you thinking of (to) your journey? 14. Yes, we are (thinking to it).

125.
PERSONAL PRONOUNS (continued).

Accusative.

Quittez-moi,	*Leave*	me	Ne me quittez pas,	*Do not leave*	me
quittez-le	,,	him	ne le quittez pas,	,,	him
quittez-la	,,	her	ne la quittez pas,	,,	her
quittez-nous	,,	us	ne nous quittez pas,	,,	us
quittez-les (m.&f.)	,,	them	ne les quittez pas,	,,	them

Dative.

Parlez-moi,	*Speak*	to me	Ne me parlez pas,	*Do not speak*	to me
parlez-lui* (m. & f.)	,,	to him (her)	ne lui* parlez pas,	,,	to him (her)
parlez-nous	,,	to us	ne nous parlez pas,	,,	us
parlez-leur*(m.&f.)	,,	to them.	ne leur* parlez pas,	,,	them

* **Y** stands for the **Dative**, *especially with reference to* **Things**:—
Consentez-y, *Consent* to it. N'y consentez pas, *Do not consent* to it.

Obs. **En** stands for the **Genitive**, *especially with reference to Things*:—
Parlez-en, *Speak* of it. N'en parlez pas, *Do not speak of it (of them)*.

With the verb in the **Imperative affirmative**, *the objective Pronoun stands after the verb (as in English), and in that case* **moi** *and* **toi** *are used instead of* **me** *and* **te**.

allez (Imperat. of aller) *go (ye)*
plutôt, *rather*
plus tôt, *sooner, earlier*
consoler, *to console, to comfort*
le pensum, *the task*
tout de suite, *at once*

dépenser, *to spend (money etc.)*
passer, *to spend (time etc.)*
enfermer, *to shut (keep) in, up*
ennuyer, *to annoy, to bore*
'haut, *high, loud*
le dîner, *the dinner.*

1. Allez chez notre pauvre voisin, portez-*lui* ces vingt francs, consolez-*le!* 2. Aime-*moi*, et je *t*'aimerai. 3. Ne *lui* donnez pas d'argent, il (elle) en dépense trop. 4. Montrez-*nous* le chemin de Bedford. 5. Je *vous* montrerai le chemin avec plaisir. 6. Vos élèves ont bien travaillé; récompensez-*les;* donnez-*leur* une récompense. 7. Mais leurs élèves ont été paresseux; *ne les* récompensez *pas*. 8. *Ne leur* donnez *pas* de récompense. 9. Enfermez-*les* plutôt, donnez-*leur* un pensum. 10. Quittez-*nous!* 11. Je *ne vous* quitterai *pas*.

126.

1. Lend me your grammar, if you please. 2. Look [at] me. 3. Don't look [at] me. 4. Here are twenty-five francs, but don't spend them at once. 5. Let us visit our old neighbour (f.), let us take (bring) her some wine, ham, cake and cherries. 6. Let us comfort her, don't let us forget her. 7. Emily has been very industrious, let us reward her. 8. These boys have not written their exercises; keep them in, give them a task instead of dinner. 9. Leave me! 10. Don't bore me! 11. Show (to) him your translation. 12. Give (to) them some money, they have none left (no more of it).

127.
PERSONAL PRONOUNS (continued).

(¹)Jean me le (la, les†) donne, John gives him, it (her, them) **to me**
(¹)Jean te le (la, les) donne,   „   him, it (her, them) **to thee**
(²)Jean le (la, les) lui donne,   „   him, it (her, them) **to him, her.**
(¹)Alice nous le(la, les) prête, Alice lends him, it (her, them) **to us**
(¹)Alice vous le(la, les) prête,   „   him, it (her, them) **to you**
(²)Alice le (la, les) leur prête,   „   him, it (her, them) **to them.**

* *The* **Dative** *is in fat type; the* **Accusative** *in Italics.*

A Verb may have two objects, a nearer (Acc.) and a remoter one (Dat.), and then —

(¹) *The pronoun in the* 1st *or* 2^{d} *person stands before the Pron. in the* 3^{d}.

(²) *If both are of the* 3^{d} *person, the Pronoun in the* Accusative *stands before the Pronoun in the* Dative.

Obs. 1. *The Reflective Pronoun* **se** *(himself, herself, itself, themselves), however, always stands first:—*
    Il se le reproche. *He reproaches himself with it.*

Obs. 2. *Two objective Pronouns cannot stand before the same Verb, unless at least one of them is of the 3d person* (le, la, les, se, en, y).

Practice:— il me le refuse, etc. Alfred me la recommande, etc. Emile me les rend, etc.

With Verbs in compound *Tenses:—*
Jean me l'a donné, etc.; Alice les leur a prêté, etc.

In **interrogative** *Sentences:—*
Jean me le donne-t-il? *or* Est-ce que Jean me le donne? etc.
Jean me l'a-t-il donné? *or* Est-ce que Jean me l'a donné? etc.

In **negative** *Sentences:—*
Il ne me le donne pas, etc.; Alice ne le leur prête pas.
Il ne me l'a pas donné, etc.; Alice ne le leur a pas prêté.

In Sentences both **negative** *and* **interrogative:—**
Ne me le donne-t-il pas? *or* Est-ce qu'il ne me le donne pas? etc.
Ne me l'a-t-il pas donné? *or* Est-ce qu'il ne me l'a pas donné? etc.

la vérité, *the truth*
le portefeuille, *pocket-book, portfolio*
dit (P. P. of dire), *said*
Catherine, *Catherine, Kate*
à condition, *on condition*
tantôt, *by and by*
il y a longtemps, *long ago*
Pâques, *(masc.) Easter*

assurer, *to assure*
refuser, *to refuse, deny*
remercier, *to thank*
rendre, *to render, to give back*
expliquer, *to explain*
renvoyer, *to send back, dismiss*
compris, *understood, comprised*
remis, *delivered, put off.*

1. Voici une poire, je te la donne. 2. Je te remercie infiniment. 3. Lui as-tu prêté ton dictionnaire? 4. Oui, je le lui ai prêté. 5. Avez-vous remis les lettres au facteur? 6. Oui, je les lui ai remises. 7. Est-ce que vous leur prêterez vos parapluies? 8. Non, nous ne les leur prêterons pas, parce que nous en aurons besoin nous-mêmes. 9. Est-ce que tu me le refuses? 10. Non, je ne te le refuse pas. 11. Vous ne m'avez pas dit la vérité. 12. Je vous assure que je vous l'ai dite. 13. Avez-vous lu son livre? 14. Non, mais je le lui ai demandé. 15. Est-ce que vous le leur avez-donné? 16. Non, nous ne le leur avons pas encore donné; mais nous le leur donnerons tantôt, s'ils promettent de nous le rendre avant Noël.

Malgré[1] les services que l'amiral Duquesne avait rendus à Louis XIV, ce prince lui refusa les titres[2] et les honneurs qu'il méritait parce qu'il était protestant. Le roi même le lui avoua.[3] „Sire, répondit Duquesne, quand j'ai combattu pour la gloire de vos armes, quand j'ai vaincu[4] vos ennemis je n'ai pas songé[5] que vous étiez d'une autre religion que moi."

1) in spite of; 2) titles; 3) confessed, owned; 4) conquered; 5) considered.

128.

1. What an interesting book! will you lend it to me? 2. I shall lend it to you with pleasure when I have* read it. 3. Has your cousin Kate read it? 4. No, she has not yet read it. 5. But I shall lend it to her, if she wishes it. 6. Why do you not give me my money? I have given it to you long ago. 7. Tell it to him. 8. Tell it to her. 9. I have already told it to her. 10. They have not told me the truth. 11. They have told it to you. 12. Have you explained the new rule to her? 13. Yes, I have explained it to her. 14. Did† she understand it. 15. Yes, she did† understand it.

*Future past. †Indefinite.

129.
PERSONAL PRONOUNS (continued).
Imperative.

Affirmative.

Montrez-*le*-moi, Show him (*it*) to me,
montrez-*le*-lui „ to him (her)
montrez-*le*-nous, „ to us,
montrez-*le*-leur, „ to them

Donnez-*la*-moi, Give her (*it*) to me,
donnez-*la*-lui, „ to (him) her
donnez-*la*-nous, „ to us,
donnez-*la*-leur, „ to them

Prêtez-*les*-moi, Lend them to me,
prêtez-*les*-lui, „ to him, etc.

Negative.

Do not show him (it) to me, etc.
ne me *le* montrez pas,
ne *le* lui montrez pas,
ne nous *le* montrez pas,
ne *le* leur montrez pas.

Do not give (her) it to me, etc.
ne me *la* donnez pas,
ne *la* lui donnez pas,
ne nous *la* donnez pas,
ne *la* leur donnez pas,

Do not lend them to me, etc.
ne me *les* prêtez pas,
ne *les* leur prêtez pas.

le service, *the service*
le relieur, *the bookbinder*
la faveur, *the favour*
la poste, *the post office*
le poste, *the post, place*

le coin, *the corner*
le plan, *the plan*
la peur, *the fear*
envoyer (Fut. enverrai) *to send*
cacher, *to hide, conceal*

relier, *to bind (books)*
garder, *to guard, to keep*
accorder, *to grant*
volontiers, *willingly*
vraiment, *truly, really*
prodigue, *prodigal*.

1. Où est votre grammaire? 2. Prêtez-*la*-moi, s'il vous plaît. 3. Je vous *la* prêterai volontiers; mais rendez-*la*-moi demain. 4. Accordez-lui cette faveur, il *la* mérite, ne *la* lui refusez pas. 5. Parlez-moi de vos affaires, ne me *les* cachez pas. 6. Montre-moi ton nouveau dictionnaire. 7. Je te *le* montrerai, quand le relieur *l*'aura relié. 8. Il y a des lettres à la poste, apportez-*les*-nous. 9. Je vous *les* aurais déjà apportées, si on me *les* avait données.

130.

1. Lend us your French-English dictionary. 2. We shall lend it to you, but do not keep it too long. 3. Show them your new book, but do not give it to them. 4. Grant us this favour, we deserve it, do not refuse it to us. 5. We have ordered several books at the bookseller's at the corner of the street, tell him to* send them to us. 6. Bring us some flowers and plants. 7. We have lent you some money, return it to us. 8. Why do you hide it from (to) me? 9. I assure you that I do not hide it from you. 10. Ask him (dat.) [for] it. 11. Do not ask her for it. 12. I have asked him for it yesterday. *de.

SECOND CONJUGATION. 71

131.

SECOND CONJUGATION:— Verbs ending in -ir.
Learn the **Present, Imperfect, Preterite** *and* **Imperative**
of finir *(see page 98), and conjugate like* finir:—

remplir, *to fill, fulfil,*   jouir, *to enjoy,*   obéir (à),   *to obey,*
bâtir,   *to build,*   punir, *to punish,*   réfléchir (à), *to reflect,*
trahir, *to betray,*   choisir, *to choose.*

Practice:— j'y réfléchis, etc.; je ne lui obéis pas, etc.; j'en jouis, etc.

l'Autrichien, *the Austrian*   la circonstance, *the cir-* embellir, *to embellish*
la colline, *the hill*   cumstance   former, *to form*
le misérable, *the wretch*   la forme, *the form*   abuser de, *to misuse*
la république, *the republic* le gouvernement, *the*   chérir, *to cherish*
la monarchie, *the mo-*   government   obtenir (irr.) *to obtain*
  narchy   l'Athénien, *the Athenian*   franchir, *to cross*
la version*, *the version,*   l'ingratitude, *f.† the un-* abolir, *to abolish*
  translation*   gratefulness   établir, *to establish*
l'ornement, *m. the orna-*   la paresse, *the idleness*   attaquer, *to attack*
  ment   vider, *to empty*   encourager, *to encou-*
la santé, *the health*   agir, *to act*.   rage.

*From a foreign language into the vernacular.
†Most Substantives in **-ude, -ure, -une** (Lat. **-udo, -ura, -una**) are feminine.

1. Quand *finirez*-vous votre version? 2. Je la *finis* à présent. 3. Vous *agissez* mal envers moi, mes amis. 4. Les fleurs *embellissent* les jardins et les prairies, elles en forment le principal ornement. 5. Si nous *obéissons* à la raison, nous *obéissons* à Dieu. 6. Voici deux tables, *choisissez*-vous la grande ou la petite? 7. *Réfléchissez*-y bien. 8. Oui, j'y *réfléchis*. 9. *Jouissez* des bienfaits de Dieu, mais n'en abusez pas. 10. Quand nous n'*obéissions* pas, on nous *punissait*. 11. Ne *jouissait*-elle pas d'une bonne santé? 12. Vous *agîtes* mal dans cette circonstance, *agissez* mieux à l'avenir.

For Practice but the Sing. Verbs in the Plur., and vice versâ.

132.

1. The Athenians used to punish (the) idleness and (the) ingratitude. 2. Whilst we were finishing our work you were reflecting. 3. We cherish our parents, and we obey them. 4. But you did not cherish yours, and (you) did not obey them. 5. At what o'clock did you finish your work? 6. We finished it at eleven o'clock. 7. Why did that wretch betray your secret? 8. He betrayed it to* obtain some money. 9. They are building a hospital on that hill. 10. Napoleon crossed the Alps by the St. Bernard and attacked the Austrians in Italy.   *to in the sence of in order to = pour.

SECOND CONJUGATION.

133.

SECOND CONJUGATION (continued).

Learn the **Future, Conditional** *and the* **Compound tenses** *of* finir *(see page 98), and conjugate like* finir:—

rougir, *to blush,*   salir, *to soil,*   réussir (à), *to succeed (in)*

l'entreprise, *f. the undertaking*
le climat, *the climate*
l'ordre, *m. the order*
le pavillon, *the flag, the garden-house*
le sommelier, *the butler*

le citoyen, *the citizen*
sérieusement, *seriously*
peut-être, *perhaps*
babiller, *to talk*
avant de (conj.), *before.*

1. Tu *obéiras* à ton père et à ta mère! 2. Vous *réfléchirez* avant d'agir et vous *réussirez* dans votre entreprise. 3. Mais les hommes qui *agissent* avant de *réfléchir* ne *réussiront* pas. 4. Quand vous *aurez franchi* les Alpes, vous *jouirez* du beau climat de l'Italie. 5. Mes neveux *réfléchiront*-ils à leur conduite? 6. Ils n'y *ont* pas encore *réfléchi*, mais ils y *réfléchiront*. 7. On vous *punirait*, mes enfants, si vous ne *finissiez* pas vos thèmes. 8. Ils *rougiraient* de leur conduite, s'ils y *réfléchissaient* sérieusement, 9. Ne *puniriez*-vous pas vos enfants, s'ils *salissaient* leurs habits? 10. Ils ne les *saliraient* plus, si vous les *punissiez*. 11. J'avais déjà *choisi* ce parapluie, quand votre ami me conseilla d'en *choisir* un autre. 12. Vous ne *réussirez* jamais, si vous ne *remplissez* pas vos devoirs plus assidûment.

For Practice put the Sing. Verbs in the Plural, and vice versâ.

134.

1. We should punish our servants, if they did not obey our orders 2. Shall you build a new house? 3. You would embellish your garden, if you built a garden-house in it. 4. He will never finish his work. 5. We should enjoy this beautiful climate, if we were not so ill. 6. Here are two horses, which* would you choose if you were in (at) my place? 7. Will the French succeed in (to) establishing† a republic? 8. I should obey him, if he were my master. 9. Has the butler filled the bottles? 10. Yes, he has filled them, but he has emptied them himself; he was very thirsty. 11. If you were wise you would have acted instead of talking.** 12. He will have finished his exercise before you. 13. He had already finished it, when I began.† 14. A good citizen will obey the laws.

*lequel.   **Infinitive.   † commençai.

135.

THIRD CONJUGATION:— **Verbs ending in -oir.**

Learn the Verb **recevoir** *(see page 100) and conjugate like* **recevoir**:—

apercevoir, *to perceive,* devoir, *to owe, to be obliged,* concevoir, *to conceive.*

le projet, *the project*
la comète, *the comet*
les étrennes, *(f.) the new year's gift*
l'idée, *f. the idea*
la lettre de change, *the bill of exchange*
la politesse, *the politeness*
l'adresse, *f. the address, the skill*
là-bas, *yonder*
le banquier, *the banker*
au lointain, *in the distance*
téméraire, *bold*
désagréable, *disagreeable*
trembler, *to tremble*
il fait froid, *it is cold* (lit. *it makes cold*)
minuit, *(m.) midnight*
convaincu, *convinced*
depuis longtemps, *long ago*
la somme, *the sum.*

1. Nous *recevions* tous les jours des visites, quand nous demeurions à Lisbonne. 2. Tu *conçois* un projet téméraire, mon ami, et tu *apercevras* trop tard que tu as eu tort. 3. Je *reçois* tous les matins des lettres de mon ami. 4. *Apercevez*-vous le feu là-bas? 5. Non, nous ne l'*apercevons* pas. 6. Donner est un plaisir, *recevoir* est souvent désagréable. 7. Je *dois* partir encore* ce soir. 8. Vous *devez* aller à l'école. 9. Vous me *devez* vingt francs. 10. *Aperçoivent*-ils ces montagnes au lointain? 11. Ce sont les Alpes. 12. Je *conçus* ce projet déjà l'année dernière. 13. En *recevant* votre lettre, je tremblai de joie. 14. Nous reçûmes avant-hier une lettre de notre ami. 15. J'*aperçus* hier une comète.

*this very.

For Practice put the Sing. Verbs in the Plur., and vice-versa.

136.

1. You owe me one pound, eleven shillings and seven pence. 2. I beg your pardon, I only[2] owe[2] you[1] one pound, seven shillings and eleven pence. 3. When I lived in Brighton, I received every day letters from my cousins. 4. It is warm. 5. He conceived really a brilliant idea. 6. Did you not perceive that he cheated you? 7. I soon perceived that the wretch betrayed me. 8. They received your answer [on] Thursday last at twelve o'clock. 9. To-morrow you will receive a bill of exchange from your banker to* pay the sum which you owe your tailor. 10. He shall receive his money, don't be afraid (have not fear). 11. They would receive their friends better, if they were not so poor. 12. You would not owe your[2] banker[2] so much[1] if you were a little less prodigal. 13. Receive everybody with politeness.

*pour.

137.

FOURTH CONJUGATION:— **Verbs ending in -re.**

Learn the **Present, Imperfect, Preterite** *and* **Imperative** *of* **vendre** *(see page 102), and conjugate like* **vendre:**—
attendre, *to wait for, to expect,* défendre, *to defend, to forbid,* entendre, *to hear, to understand,* répondre, *to reply, answer.*

Obs. Interrogatively:— Est-ce que je vends, perds? etc., and not— vends-je? perds-je? (See Exc. 81.)

le joug (g sounded), *the yoke*
le chat, *the cat*
le toit, *the roof*
la distinction, *the distinction*
immédiatement, *immediately*
le signal, *the signal*
ainsi, *thus, so;* en vain, *in vain*
le bon point, *the mark*
la rivière, *the river*
posséder, *to possess*

servir, *to serve*
promettre (je promets), *to promise*
je vous en prie! *pray!*
délivrer, *to deliver, to free*
battre (je bats), *to beat, to defeat*
battre en retraite, *to retreat*
confondre, *to confound*
comprendre (irr.), *to understand*
descendre, *to descend, come down*
perdre, *to lose.*

1. Nous *vendons* tout ce que nous possédons. 2. *Entends*-tu la musique? 3. Oui, j'*entends* les chats sur le toit. 4. *Attendez*-vous votre frère? 5. Oui, je l'*attends* ce soir. 6. Ne *confondez* pas les verbes **entendre** et **attendre**. 7. Comment *rendez*-vous le verbe anglais **to attend on** en français? 8. Par le verbe **servir**. 9. N'oubliez donc pas cette distinction. 10. J'y penserai, je vous le *promets*. 11. *Attendez* un peu, je vous en prie! 12. Pourquoi ne me *répondez*-vous pas? 13. Mais, je vous *ai répondu* depuis longtemps (Il y a longtemps que je vous *ai répondu*). 14. Celui qui ne *répond* pas à mes questions, *perdra* ses bons points. 15. Nous *attendions* en vain, personne ne *répondit* à notre lettre. 16. Nous *descendîmes* le Rhin en bateau à vapeur; et nous *attendîmes* une heure à Mayence. 17. Nous y *entendîmes* les cloches qui sonnaient. 18. Je *perdis* patience.

138.

1. Does he hear me? 2. Yes, he hears you. 3. Why then does he not wait [for] me? 4. Because he is expecting his brother. 5. They are losing patience. 6. Formerly I always used to confound these two verbs. 7. Did you hear the bells? 8. Answer him at once! 9. I (have) answered him the other day. 10. Did you answer my last questions? 11. Yes, we answered as soon as we heard you. 12. They descended from the mountain, when they heard the signal. 13. They waited only five minutes at the railway station.

139.

FOURTH CONJUGATION (continued).

Learn the **Future, Conditional** *and the* **Compound tenses** *of* **vendre** (*see page 102*) *and conjugate like* **vendre:** —
mordre, *to bite;* comprendre, *to understand.*

la perte, *the loss*	la campagne, *the country,*	muselé, *muzzled*
à perte, *at a loss*	*the country seat*	enragé, *mad*
tout le monde, *everybody*	même (adj.) *same, self*	gare! *beware, look out!*
le goût, *the taste*	même (adv.) *even*	espérer, *to hope.*

1. Je ne *vendrai* pas ma maison à perte. 2. Vous *défendrez* votre patrie. 3. Me *rendront*-ils bientôt l'argent que je leur ai prêté? 4. Quand il *sera descendu*, vous lui apporterez son déjeûner. 5. *Auriez*-vous *attendu* aussi longtemps, si vous aviez été à ma place? 6. Ils *répondront* aujourd'hui même à la lettre du ministre. 7. Lui *vendraient*-ils leur chevaux pour cent livres sterling? 8. Il y a longtemps que je vous *aurais rendu* vos livres, si vous m'aviez donné votre adresse. 9. En *défendant* notre patrie, nous n'avons fait que notre devoir. 10. Ce chien enragé *mordrait* tout le monde, s'il n'était pas muselé. 11. Vous *perdriez* le goût d'*apprendre* la langue latine, si vous n'aviez pas un si bon maître. 12. Nous *vendrions* notre maison, si nous trouvions un acheteur. 13. Nous espérons que vous ne *perdrez* pas courage. 14. *Rendez*-moi l'argent que je vous ai prêté l'année dernière.

140.

1. Will the banker sell his country seat? 2. No, he will not sell it, but he will sell his house in town. 3. I would not sell my faithful[2] dog[1] for [a] hundred pounds. 4. I would not give you five shillings for[*] it. 5. We shall learn German and Italian, and we should also learn Greek, if we had (the) time (of it). 6. Look out (beware)! that dog will bite you. 7. We shall return your books to you to-morrow. 8. Would they have waited so long, if they had been in your place? 9. Would you come down, if your father had not forbidden (it to) you? .10. We had replied to you long ago. 11. Would they not lose patience, if they had waited as long as we? 12. Our troops would defeat the enemy, if they had good officers.

[*] of.

141.
CONJUGATION OF A VERB WITH ÊTRE (see Ex. 33 Obs. & p. 107).

Infinitive: — partir, *to set out, to start.*
Pres. Part.: — partant, *Past Part.:* — parti.

Like partir conjugate: — sortir, *to go out* (with être).
dormir, *to sleep*   sentir, *to feel, smell* } (with avoir).
mentir, *to lie*   servir, *to serve, to be of use*

l'homme de bien, *the honest man*
le fer, *the iron*
les fers, *the fetters*
la douleur, *the grief, pain*
le dessert, *the dessert*
Hambourg, *Hamburgh*
le tyran, *the tyrant*
écrire, *to write*   écrivant, *writing*
consentir (à), *to consent*
le bras, *the arm*

le pied, *the foot*
ordinairement, *usually*
entrer, *to enter*
sentir bon, mauvais, *to smell nice, bad*
repartir, *to start again*
permettre, *to permit, to allow*
desservir, *to clear the table*
manquer, *to miss*
féliciter, *to congratulate*
au contraire, *on the contrary.*

1. *Consentez*-vous à ma proposition? 2. Oui, monsieur, j'y *consens* avec plaisir. 3. A quelle heure vos nièces *sortent*-elles ordinairement? 4. Elles *sortent* à trois heures, et ma sœur *sort* à quatre heures. 5. L'homme de bien *dort* en paix. 6. Vos sœurs *partent*-elles aujourd'hui? 7. Non, c'est ma cousine qui *part* aujourd'hui. 8. Je *pars* ce soir pour l'Italie. 9. Elle *sortait* quand nous entrâmes. 10. Nous *sommes* déjà *sorties* deux fois. 11. Quand nos voisines *seront parties*, nous n'aurons plus d'amies dans cette ville. 12. Il y a longtemps que ces demoiselles *sont reparties*. 13. Ces messieurs *sont*-ils déjà *sortis?* 14. Ils *seraient* déjà *sortis*, si le temps le leur permettait. 15. *Sentez*-vous des douleurs? 16. Oui, nous *sentons* des douleurs aux genoux.

142.

1. At what o'clock shall you depart for Hamburgh? 2. I should have started already if I had not missed the steamer. 3. We were going out when they entered. 4. Does he consent to your proposal? 5. No, he does not consent to it. 6. We shall not consent to obey a tyrant. 7. Do you feel that you are wrong? 8. On the contrary, I feel that I am right. 9. Have your aunts gone out this morning? 10. No, they have not yet gone out, but they will go out this evening. 11. This rose smells very sweet. 12. Does your friend feel any pain (pl.) in his* arm? 13. Has your niece slept well? 14. No, she has not slept[2] well[1], she felt (a) great pain (pl.) in her* foot.   *his, her = the.

143.
RELATIVE PRONOUNS (Pronoms relatifs).

Nom. l'homme qui* est venu, — The man who has come.
Acc. l'homme que* nous avons vu, — The man whom we have seen.
Gen. l'homme dont (de qui†) nous parlons, — The man of whom we are speaking.
Dat. l'homme à qui† nous avons parlé, — The man to whom we have spoken.

*Always qui (and never que) after prepositions:—
de qui, of whom; pour qui, for whom, etc.
†de qui and à qui only with reference to persons, not to things.

Nom. le livre qui est là, — The book which is there.
Acc. le livre que nous avons lu, — The book which we have read.
Gen. le livre dont (not de qui) nous parlons, — The book of which we are speaking.
Dat. {le livre auquel / les livres auxquels / la fleur à laquelle / les fleurs auxquelles} je donne la préférence, — The book / The books / The flower / The flowers — to which I give the preference.

le dictionnaire, the dictionary
la grammaire, (f. by except) the gram-
la bourse, the purse, exchange [mar
le musée, the museum
éprouver, to experience, try
mépriser, to despise

le garde-manger, the safe, pantry
recommander, to recommend
dicter, to dictate
aller chercher, to fetch, to send for
publier, to publish
je sais (from savoir) I know.

1. Voici le cheval *qui* a été vendu hier. 2. Voici le cheval *que* j'ai vendu hier. 3. Apportez-moi les pommes *qui* sont au garde-manger. 4. Apportez-moi aussi les pommes *que* nous avons cueillies la semaine dernière. 5. Voici la femme *dont les enfants* (subj.) sont si malades. 6. Voici aussi la femme *dont* nous avons admiré *les enfants* (obj.) 7. Je vous montrerai ce soir la grammaire *dont* je vous ai parlé et *que* je vous recommande. 8. Je ne sais pas *de qui* vous parlez. 9. Montrez-moi donc l'homme *dont* (de qui) vous parlez. 10. Je sais *à qui* vous écrivez.

144.

1. Show me the exercise which has been dictated this morning. 2. Show me also the exercise which you wrote* yesterday. 3. Here is the boy who was so lazy and whom I shall punish. 4. It is the same boy to whom I gave a task not later than yesterday, and whose conduct is generally so bad. 5. Send for the girl whose parents I have seen yesterday evening. 6. I do not know for whom you have bought the. 7. The gentleman to whom you are writing is not at home. 8. Antwerp, the museums[4] of which[1] we admired[3] so much[3], is in Belgium. 9. The servant (f.) whom you (have) recommended to us has come this morning. 10. There are five boys in this class with whom we are satisfied. *Indefinite.

145.

DEMONSTRATIVE PRONOUNS (Pronoms démonstratifs).

m. celui; f. celle, *that, he, she, the one* | m. ceux; f. celles, *those, they, the ones*
m. celui-ci; f. celle-ci, *this one* | m. ceux-ci; f. celles-ci, *those*
m. celui-là; f. celle-là, *that one* | m. ceux-là; f. celles-là, *those*.

Celui qui est content est heureux, *He who is contented is happy.*
Celui que vous récompenserez sera *He whom you will reward will be*
content, *happy.*
De tous ce thèmes, *Of all these exercises,*
je préfère {celui de votre frère, *I prefer* {*that of your brother*
{celui dont vous m'avez parlé. {*that of which you spoke to me.*

Singular.

masc. {Voici deux abricots, prenez celui-ci *Here are two apricots, take this one.*
{Non, je prendrai celui-là. *No, I shall take that one.*
fem. {Voici deux poires, prenez celle-ci. *Here are two pears, take this one.*
{Non, je prendrai celle-là. *No, I shall take that one.*

Plural.

masc. {Voici des livres, prenez ceux-ci. *Here are some books, take these.*
{Non, je prendrai ceux-là. *No, I shall take those.*
fem. {Voici des plumes, prenez celles-ci. *Here are some pens, take these.*
{Non, je prendrai celles-là. *No, I shall take those.*

Obs. Cet arbre-ci, *this tree* cet arbre-là, *that tree*
cette fleur-ci, *this flower* cette fleur-là, *that flower*
ces arbres-ci, *these trees* ces arbres-là, *those trees*
ces fleurs-ci, *these flowers* ces fleurs-là, *those flowers.*

The distinction between the English Demonstrative adjectives *this* and *that*, *these* and *those* is expressed in French by affixing ci to the nearer object and là to the remoter object.

Cet arbre-ci est plus haut que cet arbre-là, (or, to avoid repetition, que celui-là).

l'orange, *(f.) the orange* | la retenue, *the detention*
la bible, *the bible* | mis en retenue, *kept in detention*
la fabrique, *the factory* | parmi, *among*
le gamin, *the boy, urchin* | plaît (3ᵈ p. Sing. of plaire) *pleases*
le berger, *the shepherd* | il peut (3ᵈ p. Sing. of pouvoir) *he can*
le laboureur, *the husbandman* | goûter, *to taste*
la confiance, *the confidence* | comparer, *to compare*
le sort, *the fate* | ne ... rien à faire, *nothing to do*
la tragédie, *the tragedy* | à plaindre, *to pity, to be pitied*
le poète, *the poet* | occupé à, *occupied in*
l'antiquité, *f. antiquity* | verser, *to pour out*
Homère, *Homer* | traduire, *to translate*
est à, *belongs to*, sont à, *belong to* | mériter, *to deserve, to merit*
Virgile, *Virgil* | surtout, *above all.*

1. Celui *qui* travaille sera récompensé. 2. Voyez-vous ces deux écoliers? Celui *que* je préfère est occupé à traduire Charles XII. 3. Aimez-vous les oranges? 4. Oui, j'aime celles *qui* sont bien mûres. 5. Aimez-vous aussi les raisins? 6. Oui, j'aime surtout ceux *que* vous m'avez donnés à goûter. 7. J'aime les vins d'Espagne et ceux *du* Rhin. 8. J'aime aussi celui *dont* vous m'avez versé un verre. 9. Cette bible-ci a été imprimée à Londres, celle-là à Boston. 10. Cette fabrique-là est à mon frère, celle-ci à Monsieur Howard. 11. Ces hommes-ci sont heureux; ceux-là sont malheureux. 12. Ces prairies-ci sont à Monsieur Dubois, celles-là sont à la corporation.

146.

1. Those who are not contented are not happy. 2. He who does not work will be poor. 3. My friends and those of your brother [your brother's] have come. 4. He who cannot keep a secret does not deserve our confidence. 5. Those who have nothing to do are much to be pitied. 6. How do you like (find) these two pictures? 7. This one pleases me better than that. 8. What do you say of these drawings? 9. We prefer these to those. 10. Choose among these flowers, take these or those. 11. Compare thy lot with that of those wretches. 12. We prefer the tragedies of Shakspeare to those of Byron. 13. Homer and Virgil were the greatest poets of (the) antiquity, the latter was [a] Roman, the former [a] Greek.

Table showing the different meanings of ways of rendering **that**.

that, *demonstrative Adjective:*— { ce canif-là, cet homme-là, cette plume-là.

that, *demonstrative Pronoun, followed by a Genitive or by a Relative Pronoun:*— { Mon cheval est meilleur que celui de mon frère, ,, ,, celui que vous avez acheté. Votre plume est meilleure que celle de ma sœur, ,, celle que j'ai trouvée.

that (*one*), *demonstrative Pronoun without complement:*— { Mon cheval est meilleur que celui-là, Ma plume est meilleure que celle-là.

that, *demonstrative Pronoun, referring to something pointed at but not named:*— { J'ai dit cela (Acc.) Cela n'est pas vrai. (Nom.)

that, *neutral demonstr. Pronoun before the Verb* être *or before a Relat. Pron.:*— { C'est un malheur. Ce qui m'amuse.

that, *Relative Pronoun:*— { L'homme qui est venu. (Nom.) L'homme que nous avons vu venir. (Acc.)

that, *Conjunction:*— J'ai dit que c'était vrai.

147.
DEMONSTRATIVE PRONOUNS.

ceci, *this;* **cela**, *that, refer* —
(a) *to something pointed at, but not named:* —
Ceci est bon, cela n'est pas bon, *This is good, that is not good.*
(b) *to a whole preceding sentence:* — cela.
a whole following sentence: — ceci: — *as,*
Il est parti; cela ne m'étonne pas. *He has set out, that does not astonish me.*

---

ce, *this, that (it, he, she, they)* used generally (in the 3^d person only) before the Verb être: as, c'est, ce sont, c'était, ce furent, ce sera, etc.

C'est un malheur.	That *is a misfortune*
C'est pour vous que je travaille,	It *is for you that I work*
Ce sont des Italiens.	They *are Italians.*

Nom. ce qui
Acc. ce que } *that which, what;* referring to a sentence: —

Je sais ce qui me plaît,   *I know what pleases me.*
Je sais ce que je dis,   *I know what I say.*

---

la joie, *the joy, pleasure*   fort (adv.) *very*   vous dites, *you say*
la conscience, *the conscience*   inutile, *useless*   un jeu d'enfants, *child's*
fort (adj.) *strong*   possible, *possible*   *play.*

1. Je n'aime point *ceci*, donnez-moi de *cela*. 2. Que dites-vous de *cela?* 3. *Cela* est fort beau. 4. *Cela* ne me regarde pas. 5. *Ceci* est à moi, *cela* est à vous. 6. *Ceci* n'est pas un jeu d'enfants. 7. *Ce* fut une grande joie pour nous. 8. *C'est* vrai. 9. Qui est ce monsieur? 10. *C'est* mon frère. 11. *Ce qui* est utile est toujours bon. 12. *Ce que* j'ai dit, est vrai. 13. Comment trouvez-vous mon cheval? 14. J'aime mieux *celui* de votre frère. 15. Vous préférez *celui-ci* à *celui-là*. 16. *Celui qui* a une bonne conscience est heureux.

148.

1. Who has done that? 2. That is not possible. 3. How do you like (find) this? 4. Why do you buy that? 5. I have spoken of this and of that. 6. I have done that with pleasure. 7. That which is useless is always too dear. 8. That is useless. 9. Those who have a good conscience are happy. 10. Have you heard what we have said? 11. Who is this lady? 12. She is my sister. 13. To whom belong these two dogs? 14. This one belongs to William, that one to Paul. 15. Paul's dog is finer than William's, but William's is more faithful than Paul's.

149.
PASSIVE VOICE.

Learn the passive Voice of the Verb **aimer** *(see page 106) and conjugate like it:—*

examiner, *to examine;*   recevoir, *to receive;*
protéger, *to protect;*   entendre, *to hear.*

le régiment, *the regiment*
la cavalerie, *the cavalry*
le voleur, *the thief*
le vol, *the theft, the flight*
le secours, *the succour, the help*
au secours! *help!*
le paquet, *the packet, parcel*
le concitoyen, *the fellow citizen*
Pierre, *Peter*

se conduire, *to behave*
défait (Past Part. of défaire) *defeated*
flatter, *to flatter*
arrêter, *to stop*
affranchir, *to free, to prepay*
estimer, *to esteem, to value*
soutenir, *to help, to support*
St. Pétersbourg, *St. Petersburg*
satisfait, *satisfied.*

1. Ta sœur *est aimée* et *louée* de ses maîtres; mais toi, tu es *blâmé* des tiens. 2. Un homme de bien *est estimé* de ses concitoyens. 3. Ces élèves *ont*-ils *été punis* ce matin? 4. Ils n'*ont pas été punis*, mais ils *seront punis*. 5. Notre ambassadeur *a*-t-il *été* bien *reçu?* 6. Oui, il *a été* très bien *reçu*. (Oui, on l'a très bien reçu). 7. N'*êtes*-vous pas *charmés d'avoir été invités* par madame Dorand? 8. Vous *seriez aimés* de vos maîtres, si vous étiez plus attentifs. 9. Il *aura été puni* comme il l'* a mérité. 10. Ces dames *ont été attaquées* hier soir par des voleurs. 11. Mais elles crièrent au secours, leurs cris *furent entendus* par les gendarmes, et les voleurs *auraient été arrêtés*, si les gendarmes étaient arrivés assez tôt. 12. Pourquoi ces paquets n'*ont*-ils pas *été affranchis?*

* it.

150.

1. This letter has not been prepaid. 2. All citizens are protected by (the) law. 3. St. Petersburg, the capital of Russia, was (has been) founded by Peter the Great. 4. You were expected here (one expected you here). 5. You have been praised and flattered, and yet you are not satisfied. 6. Our troops would have been defeated, if they had not been supported by a regiment of cavalry. 7. These men will not be esteemed, if they continue to act thus. 8. Shall you be examined to-morrow? 9. We have already been examined yesterday. 10. I have been invited to visit him.

151.
DISJUNCTIVE PERSONAL PRONOUNS.

moi, *I, me*   nous, *we, us*
toi, *thou, thee*   vous, *you*
lui, *he, him*   eux, *m.* ⎫
elle, *she, her*   elles, *f.* ⎬ *they, them.*
     soi, *itself, one's self.*

Disjunctive *Personal Pronouns are used —*
(1) standing alone, as subject or object to a verb understood:—
     Qui a écrit cela? Moi. *Who has written that? I have.*
(2) after Prepositions:— Cela est pour toi. *That is for thee.*
     Je suis venu avec lui (elle). *I came with him (her).*
     Nous parlons malgré eux (elles). *We speak in spite of them.*

Je suis chez moi, *I am at home;*   nous sommes chez nous, *We are at*
tu es chez toi, *thou art*   „   vous êtes chez vous, *home, etc.*
il est chez lui, *he is*   „   ils sont chez eux,
elle est chez elle, *she is*   „   elles sont chez elles,
on est chez soi, *one is*   „   mes sœurs sont chez elles.

Ceci est à moi, *this is* mine,*   Cela est à nous, *that is* ours
   „   à toi,   „   thine,   „   à vous,   „   yours
   „   à lui,   „   his,   „   à eux, ⎫
   „   à elle,   „   hers,   „   à elles, ⎬ „ theirs.
* or: *This belongs to me, to thee,* etc.

(3) emphatically:—
     C'est moi, *It is I, (I am he),*   c'est nous, *it is* we
     „ toi,   „ thou,   „ vous,   „ you
     „ lui,   „ he,   ce sont eux, *m.* ⎫
     „ elle,   „ she,   „ elles, *f.* ⎬ „ they.

Est-ce moi? *It is I?* etc.   Ce n'est pas moi, *It is not I,* etc.
Moi, je prétends que c'est vrai. *As for me, I maintain it is true.*

(4) With „même":—
     moi-même, *myself*   nous-mêmes, *ourselves*
     toi-même, *thyself*   vous-mêmes, *yourselves*
     lui-même, *himself*   eux-mêmes, ⎫
     elle-même, *herself*   elles-mêmes, ⎬ *themselves.*
     soi-même, *one's self*

l'aimant, *m. the loadstone*   le maire, *the mayor*
la glace, *the ice, the looking-glass*   attirer, *to attract*
le miroir, *the mirror, the looking-*   à qui est...? *To whom belongs?*
     glass   (*whose is?*)

1. Qui a fait cela? 2. Est-ce *vous*, mon ami? 3. Non, ce n'est pas *moi*, ce sont *elles* qui ont fait cela. 4. Qui a dit cela? 5. C'est *moi* qui l'ai dit. 6. C'est *nous* qui l'avons dit. 7. Pour qui est cette pomme, pour *lui* ou pour *elle?* 8. Elle n'est ni pour *lui* ni pour *elle*, elle est pour *moi*. 9. Qui te l'a promise? 10. Ce sont *eux* qui me l'ont promise. 11. Ton père est-il *chez lui?* 12. Non, il n'est pas *chez lui*, il est sorti; je crois qu'il est allé chez le libraire qui a reçu des livres pour *lui*. 13. A qui est cela? 14. Cela n'est pas *à moi*, c'est *à elle*. 15. Mes cousins ne sont pas *chez eux*. 16. Nous finirons notre travail sans *elles*. 17. L'aimant attire le fer à *soi*. 18. Chacun pense à *soi*. 19. Nous sommes partis après *eux*. 20. Il dit qu'il est malade, *moi* je dis qu'il est en bonne santé.

Deux petits garçons, ayant trouvé une noix,[1] se la disputèrent vivement.[2] — Elle est à moi, dit l'un d'eux, car c'est moi qui l'ai vue le premier. — Non, mon cher, elle n'est pas à toi, car c'est moi qui l'ai ramassée.[3] Ils en venaient déjà aux mains[4] lorsqu'un jeune homme se plaça entre les deux petits garçons, cassa[5] la noix et dit: L'une des coquilles[6] est à celui qui le premier a vu la noix, l'autre sera pour celui qui l'a ramassée. Quant à l'amande,[7] je la garde pour prix[8] du jugement que j'ai rendu.[9]

1) nut; 2) contended for it fiercely; 3) picked up; 4) came to blows; 5) broke; 6) shells; 7) kernel; 8) reward, fee; 9) given.

152.

1. Is your mother at home? 2. No, she is not at home. 3. Who has done that, you or they? 4. It is we who have done it. 5. Whose is this money? 6. It is mine, it is not yours. 7. Shall you be at home this evening? 8. No, we shall be at our cousin Alice's. 9. Who is there? 10. It is I. 11. Whose are these books? 12. They are ours. 13. Who has related this story? 14. It is they. 15. We went out (are gone out) after them. 16. I went* yesterday to the mayor, but I did not find him at home. 17. At what o'clock shall we find your aunts at home? 18. Is it she who has broken my looking-glass? 19. We have had fewer mistakes than they, but he (*emphatic*) has had still fewer (of them). 20. I have spent several days with them in the country.

*have been.

153.

REFLECTIVE VERB.

Learn the Reflective Verb „se laver" *(see page 108) and conjugate like it* s'habiller, *to dress one's self;* se défendre, *to defend one's self.*

s'amuser, *to amuse one's self*
s'approcher de, *to approach*
se baigner, *to bathe*
se coucher, *to go to bed*
se décider à, *to determine*
s'écouler, *to flow, to pass away*
s'égarer, *to go astray*
s'exposer à, *to expose one's self to*
se fâcher contre, *to get angry wi*h
se fier à, *to trust*

se cacher, *to hide one's self*
se lever, *to rise, to get up*
se moquer de, *to laugh at*
se peigner, *to comb one's self*
se porter, *to be (in health)*
se promener, *to take a walk*
se presser de, *to hasten*
se réjouir de, *to rejoice at*
se repentir de, *to repent*
se reposer, *to rest.*

Obs. All Reflective Verbs in French are conjugated in the Compound Tenses with être, *to be.*

le bal (pl. les bals), *the ball*
le banc, *the bench, form*
la rentrée des classes, *the re-opening [of school*
rester, *to stay*

parfaitement, *perfectly, quite*
ensuite, *then, thereupon*
à droite, *to the right*
à gauche, *to the left.*

1. Comment *vous portez*-vous? 2. Nous *nous portons* parfaitement bien. 3. Comment mademoiselle votre sœur *se porte*-elle? 4. Elle ne *se porte* pas très bien, elle a mal aux dents. 5. A quelle heure *vous levez*-vous tous les matins? 6. Nous *nous levons* à six heures, ensuite nous nous *lavons*, nous *nous peignons* et nous *nous habillons*. 7. Qu'as-tu fait ce matin, mon ami? 8. Je *me suis promené* toute la matinée, puis je *me suis baigné*, et c'est ainsi que les heures *se sont écoulées*. 9. Il *s'est exposé* à un grand danger. 10. *Approchez-vous* de lui. 11. Il *se fâche*. 12. A quelle heure vos servantes *se couchent*-elles?

154.

1. How are your sisters? 2. They are quite well. 3. If they go out this evening, they will expose themselves to a great danger. 4. Go to bed early and rise early. 5. They will laugh at you, if you go astray. 6. Let us rejoice, to-day is[*] the re-opening of the schools. 7. We should rest a little, if we had walked as long as you. 8. How did you amuse yourselves (f.)? 9. I shall go to bed early, because I rose at three o'clock this morning. 10. We have walked the whole day in the forest. 11. Hide yourself. 12. Don't get angry. 13. Don't trust that man, or you will repent of it.

[*] c'est aujourd'hui.

155.

il fait froid, *it is cold*
il fait chaud, *it is warm*
il fait beau temps,* *it is fine weather*
il fait mauvais temps,* *it is bad weather*

il fait des éclairs, *it is lightning*
il fait du brouillard, *it is foggy*
il fait jour, *it is daylight*
il vaut mieux, *it is better*
il faut, *it is necessary.*

*or: Le temps est beau, mauvais.

Il me faut une grammaire grecque — I *want (must have) a Greek grammar*
il te faut une ardoise — Thou *wantest (must have) a slate*
il lui faut de l'encre — He (she) *wants (must have) some ink*
il nous faut du papier — We *want (must have) some paper*
il vous faut de la patience — You *want (must have) patience*
il leur faut des assiettes — They *want (must have) plates.*
Il me faut* retourner — I *must return*
il te faut* travailler, etc. — Thou *must work*

*or simply „il faut retourner," etc., when no mistake can arise from the omission of the pronoun.

Obs. For the construction of il faut, when the Subject is a Substantive, see Ex. 161.

le drap, *the cloth*
tout de suite, *immediately*
la cuiller, *the spoon*
la fourchette, *the fork*
souffrir, *to suffer*

le mal, *the evil*
combien y a-t-il de.. à..,
how far is it from.. to
combien y a-t-il que, *how long is it since*

il pleut, *it rains, it is raining*
il neige, *it snows, it is snowing*
payer, *to pay.*

1. Quel temps *fait-il* ce matin? 2. *Il fait* mauvais temps; *il pleut* très fort. 3. *Neige-t-il?* 4. Non, *il* ne *neige* pas dans ce moment. 5. *Il fait* des éclairs. 6. *Il vaut mieux* souffrir le mal que de* le faire. 7. Y a-t-il déjà longtemps que monsieur votre frère est revenu de son voyage? 8. Y *avait-il* beaucoup de monde au bal d'hier? 9. Combien de milles y *a-t-il* d'ici à Londres? 10. *Il me faut* un parapluie pour sortir par ce mauvais temps. 11. Combien de mètres** de drap leur faut-il? 12. Il leur faut douze mètres et demi.

*After a comparative the second verb in the infinitive is generally preceded by de.   ** 1 mètre = 1¹/₁₀ yard.

156.

1. What o'clock is it? 2. It is five o'clock, it is daylight. 3. Is the weather fine? 4. No, it is bad weather, it snows and it rains. 5. It is better [to] stay at home. 6. Has your cousin been living here a long time? 7. How far is it from here to Brighton? 8. He wants a dictionary. 9. They want several books. 10. He must set off to-day for Dover. 11. It is necessary to obey. 12. Is it necessary to pay at once? 13. What do they want? 14. They want some coffee and (some) sugar

SUBJUNCTIVE OF AUXILIARY VERBS.

157.

Learn the **Pres. & Imperf. Subj.** *of* **avoir** *and* **être** (pp. 90-93).

The Subjunctive mood is used in dependent *clauses:* —
(1) *When the Verb in the* principal *clause expresses* —
  a wish, command, order: — désirer, *to desire;* ordonner, *to order;* vouloir, *to wish, to want.*
  a doubt, negation*: — douter, *to doubt;* ne pas croire, *not to believe.*
  joy, sorrow, fear, astonishment: — se réjouir, *to rejoice*, être fâché, *to be sorry;* craindre, *to fear;* s'étonner, *to be astonished.*
(2) *after many Impersonal Verbs:* — il faut, *it is necessary;* il convient, *it is convenient;* il importe, *it is important;* il vaut mieux, *it is better.*
(3) *after Superlatives:* — le plus grand, le premier, le dernier.
(4) *after certain Conjunctions:* — quoique, *although;* afin que, *in order that;* quoi que, *whatever;* à moins que, *unless.*
  *Verbs of thinking and believing used interrogatively or negatively.

Obs. Que (Relat. Pron. and Conjunction) is never omitted in French: —
Le cheval que vous avez acheté.   *The horse (that) you have bought.*
Je crois qu'il a raison.   *I think (that) he is right.*

Vouloir *to wish, to want*   **Croire** *to believe, to think*
je veux,   nous voulons,   je crois,   nous croyons
tu veux,   vous voulez,   tu crois,   vous croyez
il veut,   ils veulent.   il croit,   ils croient.
reconnaissant, *grateful*   obéissant, *obedient*
la dépense, *the expense*   impossible, *impossible.*

1. Dieu veut que tous les hommes *soient* bons. 2. Le maître désire que nous *soyons* attentifs. 3. Je doute que cela *soit* vrai. 4. Nous doutons qu'il *ait* raison. 5. Il est juste que les enfants *soient* reconnaissants envers leurs parents. 6. Croyez-vous qu'il *soit* heureux? 7. Non, je ne crois pas qu'il *soit* heureux. 8. Mais je crois que son frère est heureux. 9. Je m'étonne que tu *aies* moins de fautes que moi. 10. Il faut qu'ils soient riches pour faire tant de dépenses.

158.

1. I doubt if (that) my brother has (the) time to accompany you. 2. It is just that you should be obedient to your parents. 3. Do you think (that) they are rich? 4. No, I do not think (that) they are rich, but we think they are happy. 5. It is better that you should be here this afternoon. 6. They have been disobedient, it is just that they should be punished. 7. I do not think (that) he has your letter. 8. Although he has money, he is not satisfied. 9. Our parents wish us to be (wish that we should be) attentive. 10. I do not think that you are right.

SUBJUNCTIVE OF AUXILIARY VERBS. 87

159.
SUBJUNCTIVE OF AUXILIARY VERBS (see pp. 90—93).
Learn the **Perfect** *and* **Pluperfect** *of* avoir *and* être.
Sequence of Tenses.

{ Il faut que j'aie, (que je sois),   *I must have (be).*
{ Il faudra que j'aie (que je sois), *I shall be obliged to have (to be).*
{ Il fallait (fallut) que j'eusse,   *I was obliged to have.*
{ Il fallait (fallut) que je fusse,   *I was obliged to be.*
{ Il faudrait que j'eusse,   *I ought to have, etc.*

Il faut que je travaille,   *I have to work (I must work)*
Il faudra que je travaille,   *I shall have to work.*
Il fallut que je travaillasse, *I had to work.*

Elle veut que j'aie (je sois),   *She wishes me to have (be).*
Elle veut que tu aies (sois),   *She wishes thee to have (be).*
Elle voulait que j'eusse (je fusse), *She wished me to have (be).*

For practice conjugate the above in all persons.
jusque (*prep.*)   }   tôt,   }
jusqu'à ce que (*conj.*) } *until*   de bonne heure, } *early.*

1. Il *faut* que nous *ayons* patience. 2. Il *fallut* que nous *eussions* patience. 3. Je *suis* content de ton thème, quoiqu'il y *ait* quelques fautes. 4. Je *fus* content de son thème, quoiqu'il y *eût* quelques fautes. 5. *Ayez* patience jusqu'à ce que le train *soit* arrivé. 6. Ils *attendirent* jusqu'à ce que le train *fut* arrivé. 7. *Sois* obéissant et reconnaissant, afin que tu *sois* digne de tes parents. 8. Elle ne *fut* pas heureuse, quoiqu'elle *fût* riche. 9. Tu n'*étais* jamais content, quoique tu *eusses* toujours assez d'argent. 10. Le maître *désirait* que vous *fussiez* attentives. 11. Je *regrettai* que tu n'*eusses* pas le temps de m'accompagner.

160.
1. You must have patience. 2. I shall wait until the trains have arrived. 3. They were not happy although they were very rich. 4. He was never satisfied although he had money enough. 5. Your parents wish you to be happy. 6. We were sorry that they had not time to accompany us. 7. We did not doubt that they were right. 8. I tell you that in order that you may be satisfied. 9. It would have been necessary for me to (that I should) have a dictionary. 10. Let us be obedient in order that we may be worthy of the affection of our parents. 11. It was impossible that we should have arrived early enough.

161.
SUBJUNCTIVE OF THE FOUR REGULAR CONJUGATIONS.

Learn the **Present** *Subjunctive of* **parler, finir, recevoir** *and* **vendre** *(see pp. 96—102) and conjugate —*

travailler, *to work;* accomplir, *to accomplish;* apercevoir, *to perceive:* défendre, *to defend, to forbid.*

Il faut que je travaille (que j'aie tra-   *I must work (have worked)*
vaillé),
Il faudra que je travaille,   *I shall have to work, etc.*
Il faut (faudra) que l'écolier travaille,   *The scholar must (will have to) work.*

When the Subject is a **Pronoun,** „il faut" *can be construed in two ways:—*

Il (me) faut étudier (see Ex. 155) } *I must study;*
or Il faut que j'étudie

But if the Subject is a **Substantive,** *the latter construction only is admissible:—*

Il faut que l'élève étudie,   *The pupil must study.*

le vœu, *the vow, wish*   de manière que *(Subj.) so that*
le bien, *the good, property*   s'accomplir, *to be fulfilled*
bien, *well, very*   partager, *to divide, to share*
désirer, souhaiter, *to wish*   le procès, *the law-suit.*

1. Il faut que je *finisse* mes thèmes ce soir. 2. Il faut qu'il *descende.* 3. Il désire que nous *chantions.* 4. Nous souhaitons que vos vœux s'*accomplissent.* 5. Je crains que vous ne *receviez* de mauvaises nouvelles. 6. Tu exiges qu'il te *rende* tes livres. 7. Le maître ordonne que vous *finissiez* vos thèmes. 8. Je veux que vous me *répondiez* franchement. 9. Il est juste que vous *partagiez* votre bien avec les pauvres. 10. Je ne crois pas qu'il *finisse* son thème avant moi. 11. Dieu veut que nous *aimions* nos ennemis et que nous leur *pardonnions.* 12. Nous sommes étonnés qu'ils *entendent* si bien l'anglais.

162.

1. I am glad that you enjoy (of) such a* good health. 2. I wish that their wishes may be fulfilled. 3. We do not think that they will finish their work before you. 4. I am astonished that he understands German so well. 5. They wish you to (wish that you) sing. 6. Is it possible that you should spend so much money in books? 7. Do you think that I may succeed? 8. My master wishes me to work. 9. It is necessary that we obey our parents. 10. Our friend wishes that we receive our reward. 11. Speak so that every one may understand you.   **such a = a so.*

163.

SUBJUNCTIVE (continued).

Learn the Subjunctive **Imperfect, Perfect** *and* **Pluperfect** *of the four Regular Conjugations, (pp. 96—103) and conjugate:—*
étudier, *to study;* choisir, *to choose;* devoir, *to owe;* répondre, *to answer*

le rempart, *the rampart*	sur-le-champ, *immediately*
plût à Dieu, *would to God*	ordonner (à), *to order, command*
étonnant, *astonishing*	défendre, *to defend, to forbid*
davantage (*never followed by* que) *more*	avant *(prep.)* avant que *(conj. with subj.)* } *before.*

1. Le général ordonna que la garnison *défendît* les remparts de la ville. 2. Je désirerais qu'il *arrivât* ce matin. 3. J'avais peur que nous ne *reçussions* de mauvaises nouvelles de Londres. 4. Il faillait qu'il *partît* sur-le-champ. 5. Plût à Dieu qu'ils *eussent* fait leur devoir. 6. Nous accompagnâmes mon frère, afin qu'il ne s'*égarât* pas. 7. Il souhaitait que je lui *répondisse* tout de suite. 8. Il fut bien étonnant qu'il *perdît* son procès. 9. Il était temps que vous *finissiez* votre lettre. 10. Nous désirions qu'il *étudiât* davantage.

164.

1. The master ordered that the pupil should finish his exercise. 2. I was afraid that he would receive bad news from his parents. 3. Would to God that he had left the town. 4. They accompanied their friends in order that they might not go astray. 5. It was astonishing that he should betray his best friends. 6. They wished that we should reply to them by return of post. 7. The generals ordered the troops to (that the troops should) cross the bridge. 8. You went* out before we arrived. 9. We studied much, though we were ill. 10. My brother did not find his book, although he looked for it everywhere. †Indef.

The Verbs.

AUXILIARY VERBS.

AVOIR, to have.

	INFINITIVE.			PARTICIPLE.
Pres.	avoir, *to have,*		*Pres.*	ayant, *having,*
Past.	avoir eu, *to have had.*		*Past.*	eu, *had.*

	INDICATIVE.			SUBJUNCTIVE.
PRESENT.	j' ai, *I have, etc.* tu as il a nous avons vous avez ils ont		**PRESENT.**	*[(should) have, etc.* que j' aie, *that I may* que tu aies qu'il ait que nous ayons que vous ayez qu'ils aient
IMPERFECT.	j' avais, *I had, etc.* tu avais il avait nous avions vous aviez ils avaient			
PRETERITE.	j' eus, *I had, etc.* tu eus il eut nous eûmes vous eûtes ils eurent		**IMPERFECT.**	*[(should) have, etc.* que j' eusse, *that I might* que tu eusses qu'il eût que nous eussions que vous eussiez qu'ils eussent

VERBS.

	INDICATIVE.		SUBJUNCTIVE.
P. INDEFINITE.	j' ai eu, *I have had*, etc. tu as eu il a eu nous avons eu vous avez eu ils ont eu	PERFECT.	*that I may have had*, etc. que j' aie eu que tu aies eu qu' il ait eu que nous ayons eu que vous ayez eu qu' ils aient eu
PLUPERFECT.	j' avais eu, *I had had*, etc. tu avais eu il avait eu nous avions eu vous aviez eu ils avaient eu		
P. ANTERIOR.	j' eus eu, *I had had*, etc. tu eus eu il eut eu nous eûmes eu vous eûtes eu ils eurent eu	PLUPERFECT.	*that I might have had*, etc. que j' eusse eu que tu eusses eu qu' il eût eu que nous eussions eu que vous eussiez eu qu' ils eussent eu
FUTURE PRESENT.	j' aurai, *I shall have*, etc. tu auras il aura nous aurons vous aurez ils auront	PRESENT.	CONDITIONAL. j' aurais, *I should have*, etc. tu aurais il aurait nous aurions vous auriez ils auraient
FUTURE PAST.	j' aurai eu, *I shall have* tu auras eu [*had*, etc. il aura eu nous aurons eu vous aurez eu ils auront eu	PAST.	*I should have had*, etc j' aurais eu tu aurais eu il aurait eu nous aurions eu vous auriez eu ils auraient eu

IMPERATIVE.

aie, *have (thou)*
qu'il ait, *let him have*

ayons, *let us have*
ayez, *have (ye)*
qu'ils aient, *let them have.*

ÊTRE, *to be.*

	INFINITIVE.		PARTICIPLE.
Pres.	être, *to be*	*Pres.*	étant, *being*
Past.	avoir été, *to have been*	*Past.*	été, *been*

	INDICATIVE.		SUBJUNCTIVE.
PRESENT.	je suis, *I am,* etc. tu es il est nous sommes vous êtes ils sont	**PRESENT.**	*that I may (should) be,* etc. que je sois que tu sois qu' il soit que nous soyons que vous soyez qu' ils soient
IMPERFECT.	j' étais, *I was,* etc. tu étais il était nous étions vous étiez ils étaient		
PRETERITE.	je fus, *I was,* etc. tu fus il fut nous fûmes vous fûtes ils furent	**IMPERFECT.**	*that I might (should) be,* etc. que je fusse que tu fusses qu' il fût que nous fussions que vous fussiez qu' ils fussent
P. INDEFINITE.	*I have been,* etc. j' ai été tu as été il a été nous avons été vous avez été ils ont été	**PERFECT.**	*that I may have been,* etc. que j' aie été que tu aies été qu' il ait été que nous ayons été que vous ayez été qu' ils aient été
PLUPERFECT.	*I had been,* etc. j' avais été tu avais été il avait été nous avions été vous aviez été ils avaient été		

	INDICATIVE.		SUBJUNCTIVE.
P. ANTERIOR.	*I had been,* etc. j' eus été tu eus été il eut été nous eûmes été vous eûtes été ils eurent été	PLUPERFECT.	*that I might have been,* etc. que j' cusse été que tu eusses été qu' il eût été que nous eussions été que vous eussiez été qu' ils cussent été
FUTURE PRESENT.	je serai, *I shall be,* etc. tu seras il sera nous serons vous serez ils seront	PRESENT.	CONDITIONAL. je serais, *I should be,* etc. tu serais il serait nous serions vous seriez ils seraient
FUTURE PAST.	*I shall have been,* etc. j' aurai été tu auras été il aura été nous aurons été vous aurez été ils auront été	PAST.	*I should have been,* etc. j' aurais été tu aurais été it aurait été nous aurions été vous auriez été ils auraient été

IMPERATIVE.

sois, *be* (thou)
qu'il soit, *let him be*

soyons, *let us be*
soyez, *be* (ye)
qu'ils soient, *let them be.*

Regular Verbs. Formation of Tenses.

There are four Regular Conjugations, distinguished by their Infinitive Terminations:

1. -er (aimer, *to love*). 2. -ir (finir, *to finish*). 3. -oir (recevoir, *to receive*). 4. -re (vendre, *to sell*).

Obs. Strictly speaking there are only three regular conjugations, the Verbs in -oir being all irregular, since a part of their stem is dropped in several Tenses and Persons. To avoid confusion, however, the old classification is retained, according to which the seven Verbs in -evoir represent the Regular Third Conjugation.

In order to conjugate a Verb it is necessary to know its Principal Parts from which the *Derived Parts* are formed thus

	I.	II.	III.	IV.
	aim-er	fin-ir	recev-(ol)r	vend-r(e)
(a) from the Infinitive				
1) the *Future Pres.* by adding the inflections -ai, -as, -a; -ons, -ez, -ont[1]).	1. aimer-ai, -ons 2. - -as, -ez 3. - -a,[2]) -ont	finir-ai, -ons - -as, -ez - -a, -ont	recevr-ai, -ons - -as, -ez - -a, -ont	vendr-ai, -ons - -as, -ez - -a, -ont
2) the *Conditional Pres.* by adding the inflections -ais, -ais, -ait; -ions, iez, aient.	1. aimer-ais, -ions 2. - -ais, -iez 3. - -ait, -aient	finir-ais, -ions - -ais, -iez - -ait, -aient	recevr-ais, -ions - -ais, -iez - -ait, -aient	vendr-ais, -ions - -ais, -iez - -ait, -aient
(b) from the Pres. Part.	aim-ant	fin-iss-ant	recev-ant	vend-ant
1) the *Pres. Indic. Plur.* by changing -ant into -ons, -ez, -ent.	1. aim-ons 2. - -ez 3. - -ent	fin-iss-ons - -iss -ez - -iss -ent	recev-ons - -ez reçoiv-ent	vend-ons - -ez - -ent
2) the *Imperfect Indic.* by changing -ant into -ais, -ais, -ait; -ions, iez, aient.	1. aim-ais, -ions 2. - -ais, -iez 3. - -ait, -aient	fin-iss -ais, -iss -ions - -iss -ais, -iss -iez - -iss -ait, -iss -aient	recev-ais, -ions - -ais, -iez - -ait, -aient	vend-ais, -ions - -ais, -iez - -ait, -aient
3) the *Pres. Subjunctive* by changing -ant into -e, -es, -e; -ions, -iez, -ent.	1. aim-e, -ions 2. - -es, -iez 3. - -e,[3]) -ent	fin-iss -e, -iss -ions - -iss -es, -iss -iez - -iss -e, -iss -ent	reçoiv-e*, recev-ions - -es, -iez - -e, reçoiv-ent *see obs. to (d).	vend-e, -ions - -es, -iez - -e, -ent

VERBS.

§ 79. (c) fr. the Past Part.   aim-é   fin-i   reç-u   vend-u

1) all *Compound Tenses* with avoir or être

	aimé.	fini.	reçu.	vendu.
j'ai				
j'avais				
j'eus				
j'aurai				
j'aurais				

2) the *Passive Voice* with être

	aimé *or* aimée.	fini *or* finie.	reçu *or* reçue.	vendu *or* vendue.
je suis				
j'étais				
je fus				
je serai				
je serais				

(d) from the Pres. Indicative.

1.	aim-e, -ons	fin-is, -issons	reç-ois, recev-ons	vend-s, -ons
2.	- -es, -ez	- -is, -issez	- -ois, -ez	- -s, -ez
3.	- -e², -ent	- -it, -issent	- -ois, reçoi-vent	- -², -ent

1) the *Imperative* by dropping the Pers. Pron.

1.	aim-ons	fin-iss -ons	recev-ons	vend-ons
2.	aim-e*, -ez	fin-is, -iss -ez	reç-ois, - -ez	vend-s, - -ez

*-s dropped in the 1st Conj.

also the *Pres. Subj. Sing.* & the 3ᵈ pers. pl. of the 3ᵈ Conj. & of nearly all Irr. Verbs; by cutting off -nt of the 3ᵈ p. pl.

1.	aim-e,	fin-isse,	1. reçoiv-e,	vend-e,
2.	- -es,	- -isses,	2. - -es,	- -es,
3.	- -t,	- -it,	3. - -e, reçoiv-ent	- -e,

(e) fr. the Preterite (Défini) 2ᵈ pers. Sing.

1.	aim-ai, -âmes	fin-is, -îmes	reç-us, -ûmes	vend-is, -îmes
2.	- -as, -âtes	- -is, -îtes	- -us, -ûtes	- -is, -îtes
3.	- -a², -èrent	- -it, -irent	- -ut, -urent	- -it, -irent

the *Imperfect Subjunctive* by changing the final s into -sse, -sses, -̂t -ssions, -ssiez -ssent.

1.	aim-asse, -assions	fin-isse, -issions	reç-usse, -ussions	vend-isse, -issions
2.	- -asses, -assiez	- -isses, -issiez	- -usses, -ussiez	- -isses, -issiez
3.	- -ât, -assent	- -it, -issent	- -ût, -ussent	- -it, -issent

1) These tense-inflections of the Future and Conditional are derived from the *Pres.* and *Imperf.* of avoir (ai and av-ais) respectively. (See Introd. § 10, last section).

2) The person-inflection -t is always dropped after the final stem-consonants d, t, c, after e mute and a (*Imperf. Subj.* excepted).

A. ACTIVE VOICE.

First Conjugation: **aim-er,** *to love.*

	INFINITIVE.		PARTICIPLE.
Pres.	**aim-er,** *to love*	*Pres.*	**aim-ant,** [1] *loving*
Past.	avoir **aim-é,** *to have loved*	*Past.*	**aim-é,** f. **-ée,** [2] *loved*

	INDICATIVE.		SUBJUNCTIVE.
PRESENT.	*I love, I am loving, I do love,* [etc. j' aime [3] tu aimes il aime nous aimons vous aimez ils aiment	**PRESENT.**	*that I may (should) love, etc.* que j' aime que tu aimes qu' il aime que nous aimions que vous aimiez qu' ils aiment
IMPERFECT.	*I loved, I was loving, I did* [*love, etc.* j' aimais [4] tu aimais il aimait nous aimions vous aimiez ils aimaient		
PRETERITE.	j' aimai, [5] *I loved, etc.* tu aimas il aima nous aimâmes vous aimâtes ils aimèrent	**IMPERFECT.**	*that I might (should) love, etc.* que j' aimasse [6] que tu aimasses qu' il aimât que nous aimassions que vous aimassiez qu' ils aimassent
INDEFINITE.	j' ai aimé, *I have loved, etc.* tu as aimé, etc.	**PERFECT.**	*that I may have loved, etc.* que j' aie aimé, que tu aies aimé, etc.

VERBS. 97

	INDICATIVE.		SUBJUNCTIVE.
PLUPERFECT.	j' avais aimé, *I had loved*, etc. tu avais aimé, etc.		
P. ANTERIOR.	j' eus aimé, *I had loved*, etc. tu eus aimé, etc.	PLUPERFECT.	that *I might have loved*, etc. que j' eusse aimé que tu eusses aimé, etc.
FUTURE PRESENT.	j' aimerai, *I shall love*, etc. tu aimeras il aimera nous aimerons vous aimerez ils aimeront	PRESENT.	CONDITIONAL. j' aimerais, *I should love*, tu aimerais [etc. il aimerait nous aimerions vous aimeriez ils aimeraient
FUTURE PAST.	[*loved*, etc. j' aurai aimé, *I shall have* tu auras aimé, etc.	PAST.	*I should have loved*, etc. j' aurais aimé tu aurais aimé, etc.

IMPERATIVE.

aime, *(love thou)*
(qu'il aime, *let him love*)

aimons, *let us love*
aimez, *love (ye)*
(qu'ils aiment, *let them love*).

---

1. From the Lat. Part. Pres. acc. **amantem** (not from the Nom.; see Introd. § 19).
2. From the Lat. Part. Perf. Pass. **amatus.** (The Lat. ending -atus becomes é in Fr., comp. clericatus = clergé.)
3. From the Lat. Pres. Indicat.
4. From the Lat. Imperf. -a(b)am, a(b)as.
5. From the Lat. Perf. -a(v)i, by the dropping of v.
6. From the Lat. contracted Pluperf. Subj. **-assem.**

} see Introd. § 21.

7

Second Conjugation: finir, *to finish.*

	INFINITIVE.		PARTICIPLE.
Pres.	fin-ir, *to finish*	*Pres.*	fin-iss-ant, *finishing*
Past.	avoir fin-i, *to have finished*	*Part.*	fin-i, f. -ie, *finished*

	INDICATIVE.		SUBJUNCTIVE.
PRESENT.	*I finish, I am finishing, I do* [*finish,* etc.] je finis tu finis il finit nous finissons vous finissez ils finissent	**PRESENT.**	*that I may (should) finish,* etc. que je finisse que tu finisses qu' il finisse que nous finissions que vous finissiez qu' ils finissent
IMPERFECT.	*I finished, I was finishing, I* [*did finish,* etc.] je finissais tu finissais il finissait nous finissions vous finissiez ils finissaient		
PRETERITE.	je finis, *I finished,* etc. tu finis il finit nous finîmes vous finîtes ils finirent	**IMPERFECT.**	*that I might (should) finish,* etc. que je finisse que tu finisses qu' il finît que nous finissions que vous finissiez qu' ils finissent
INDEFINITE.	j' ai fini, *I have finished,* etc. tu as fini, etc.	**PERFECT.**	*that I may have finished,* etc. que j' aie fini que tu aies fini, etc.
PLUPERFECT.	*I had finished,* etc. j' avais fini tu avais fini, etc.		

VERBS.

	INDICATIVE.		SUBJUNCTIVE.
P. ANTERIOR.	j' eus fini, *I had finished*, etc. tu eus fini, etc.	PLUPERFECT.	*that I might have finished* etc. que j' eusse fini que tu eusses fini, etc.
FUTURE PRESENT.	je finirai, *I shall finish*, etc. tu finiras il finira nous finirons vous finirez ils finiront	PRESENT.	CONDITIONAL. je finirais, *I should finish*, tu finirais [etc. il finirait nous finirions vous finiriez ils finiraient
FUT. PAST.	*I shall have finished.* etc. j' aurai fini tu auras fini, etc.	PAST.	*I should have finished*, etc. j' aurais fini tu aurais fini, etc.

IMPERATIVE.

finis, *finish (thou)*
(qu'il finisse, *let him finish*)

finissons, *let us finish*
finissez, *finish (ye)*
(qu'ils finissent, *let them finish*.)

Obs. The regular form of the Second Conjugation is derived from Lat. *Inchoative (Inceptive)* Verbs, as flor-esc-o, the character esc of which became in French iss, — the character of the regular Second Conjugation.

The ss of -iss- is retained before vowel-inflections only; in all other cases it is dropped:

fin-iss-ant, fin-iss-ons, fin-iss-ais, que je fini-ss-e, etc.
but fini-r, je fini-s, il fini-t, je fini-rai, etc.

A great many Verbs which are not derived from Lat. inchoatives or from Latin at all, take the Character -iss. For the few which do not take it see §§ 93 and 94.

VERBS.

Third Conjugation: **recevoir,** *to receive.* (see Obs.)

	INFINITIVE.		PARTICIPLE.
Pres.	rec(ev)-oir, *to receive*	*Pres.*	rec(ev)-ant, *receiving*
Past.	avoir reç-u, *to have received*	*Past.*	reç-u, f. -ue, *received*

	INDICATIVE.		SUBJUNCTIVE.
PRESENT.	*I receive, I am receiving, I do* je reçois [*receive,* etc. tu reçois il reçoit nous recevons vous recevez ils reçoivent	**PRESENT.**	*that I may (should) receive,* etc. que je reçoive que tu reçoives qu' il reçoive que nous recevions que vous receviez qu' ils reçoivent
IMPERFECT.	*I received, I was receiving, I did* je recevais [*receive,* etc. tu recevais il recevait nous recevions vous receviez ils recevaient		
PRETERITE.	je reçus, *I received,* etc. tu reçus il reçut nous reçûmes vous reçûtes ils reçurent	**IMPERFECT.**	*that I might (should) receive,* que je reçusse [etc. que tu reçusses qu' il reçût que nous reçussions que vous reçussiez qu' ils reçussent
INDEFINITE.	j' ai reçu, *I have received,* etc. tu as reçu, etc.	**PERFECT.**	*that I may have received,* etc. que j' aie reçu que tu aies reçu, etc.
PLUPERFECT.	*I have received,* etc. j' avais reçu tu avais reçu, etc.		
ANTERIOR.	*I had received,* etc. j' eus reçu tu eus reçu, etc.	**PLUPERFECT.**	*that I might have received,* etc. que j' eusse reçu que tu eusses reçu, etc.

VERBS. 101

	INDICATIVE.		
FUTURE PRES.	je recevrai, *I shall receive,* tu recevras [etc. il recevra nous recevrons vous recevrez ils recevront	**PRESENT.**	**CONDITIONAL.** je recevrais, *I should receive,* tu recevrais [etc. il recevrait nous recevrions vous recevriez ils recevraient
FUTURE PAST.	*I shall have received,* etc. j' aurai reçu tu auras reçu, etc.	**PAST.**	*I should have received,* etc. j' aurais reçu tu aurais reçu, etc.

IMPERATIVE.

                                               recevons,   *let us receive*
reçois, *receive (thou)*   recevez,   *receive (ye)*
(qu'il reçoive, *let him receive*)   (qu'ils reçoivent, *let them receive*)

    Obs. 1. Three stems must be distinguished in Verbs of this Conjugation:

* **recev-** for the *Pres. Part. and its derived Tenses:* —
    recev-ant, recev-ons, recev-ais, etc.;
(but **recevr-** for the *Fut. and Condit.:* — recevr-ai, recevr-ais, etc.)

***reçoi(v)-** for the Sing. and 3ᵈ. p. plur. of the *Pres. Indic.* and *Subj.* and of the *Imperative:*
    je reçoi-s, il reçoi-t, que je reçoiv-e, reçoi-s, etc.

reç- for the *Past. Part.* Preterite and *Imperf. Subj.:*
    reç-u, je reç-us, je reç-usse, etc.

*The real difference between these two stems is that **recev-** stands before sonorous inflections only — ant, ons, ais, etc.; whilst the strengthened stem **reçoi(v)-** stands before mute inflections e, es, ent; s, t; (v dropped before consonants: reçoi-(v)s, -(v)t), on the same principle as
ten-ir = tien-s, tienn-ent; men-er = mèn-e, mèn-ent; appel-er = appell-e, etc.

Verbs ending in **-cvoir** only are conjugated like **recevoir**: as, devoir, *to owe, to be obliged;* apercevoir, *to perceive;* concevoir, *to conceive;* décevoir, *to deceive;* percevoir, *to collect, (taxes* etc.)

    Obs. 2. devoir, takes a circumflex in the Past. Part. **dû,** *masc.* but *fem.* **due,** and *plur.* **dus** without circumflex.

    Obs. 3. In Verbs ending in **-evoir** the **c** takes a *cedilla* before **o** and **u**.

Fourth Conjugation: vendre, *to sell.*

	INFINITIVE.		PARTICIPLE.
Pres.	vend-re, *to sell*	*Pres.*	vend-ant, *selling*
Past.	avoir vend-u, *to have sold*	*Part.*	vend-u, f. -ue, *sold*

	INDICATIVE.		SUBJUNCTIVE.
PRESENT.	*I sell, I am selling, I do sell,* je vends [etc. tu vends il vend [1]) nous vendons vous vendez ils vendent	**PRESENT.**	*that I may (should) sell,* etc. que je vende que tu vendes qu' il vende que nous vendions que vous vendiez qu' ils vendent
IMPERFECT.	*I sold, I was selling, I did sell,* je vendais [etc. tu vendais il vendait nous vendions vous vendiez ils vendaient		
PRETERITE.	je vendis, *I sold,* etc. tu vendis il vendit nous vendîmes vous vendîtes ils vendirent	**IMPERFECT.**	*that I might (should) sell,* etc. que je vendisse que tu vendisses qu' il vendît que nous vendissions que vous vendissiez qu' ils vendissent
INDEFINITE.	j' ai vendu, *I have sold,* etc. tu as vendu, etc.	**PERFECT.**	*that I may have sold,* etc. que j' aie vendu que tu aies vendu, etc.
PLUPER-FECT.	j' avais vendu, *I had sold,* etc. tu avais vendu, etc.		

VERBS. 103

	INDICATIVE.		SUBJUNCTIVE.
ANTERIOR.	j' eus vendu, *I had sold*, etc. tu eus vendu, etc.	PLUPER- FECT.	*that I might have sold*, etc. que j' eusse vendu que tu eusses vendu, etc.
FUTURE PRESENT.	je vendrai, *I shall sell*, etc. tu vendras il vendra nous vendrons vous vendrez ils vendront	PRESENT.	CONDITIONAL. je vendrais, *I should sell*, tu vendrais [etc. ils vendrait nous vendrions vous vendriez ils vendraient
FUTURE PAST.	[*sold*, etc. j' aurai vendu, *I shall have* tu auras vendu, etc.	PAST.	*I should have sold*, etc. j' aurais vendu, tu aurais vendu, etc.

IMPERATIVE.

vends, *sell (thou)*
(qu'il vende, *let him sell*)
vendons, *let us sell*
vendez, *sell (ye)*
(qu'ils vendent, *let them sell*.)

---

1) The person-inflection · t is always dropped after dentals (d, t) and after c:

perd-re; il perd-,   *but* romp-re,   il romp-t
vainc-re, il vainc-,   plai-re,   il plai-t
mett-re. il met-,   construi-re, il construi-t, etc.

104   VERBS.

α. The rules for conjugating Verbs *interrogatively* and *negatively* are the same as those given for Auxiliary Verbs, §§ 74—76:

Obs. For the sake of euphony the 1st pers. sing. of the Pres. Indic. takes an acute accent on the final e: j'aime, *interrogatively* aimé-je?

I do not love, etc.	*Do I love?*	*Do I not love?* etc.	
Je n'aime pas	aimé-je?	N'aimé-je pas?	*I have not loved,* etc.
tu n'aimes pas	aimes-tu?	n'aimes-tu pas?	Je n'ai pas aimé, etc.
il n'aime pas	aime-t-il?	n'aime-t-il pas?	*Have I loved?*
nous n'aimons pas	aimons-nous?	n'aimons-nous pas?	ai-je aimé? etc.
vous n'aimez pas	aimez-vous?	n'aimez-vous pas?	*Have I not loved?* etc.
ils n'aiment pas	aiment-ils?	n'aiment-ils pas?	N'ai-je pas aimé? etc.

β. REMARKS ON SOME PECULIARITIES OF THE FIRST AND SECOND CONJUGATIONS.

1) In Verbs ending in **-ger**: as, **manger**, *to eat*, an **e** mute is inserted between the stem and the inflection, whenever the latter begins with **a** or **o**; as,

mang-er	je mang-e, n. mange-ons	je mange-ais, n. mang -ions
mang-e-ant	tu - -es, v. mang-ez	tu - -e-ais, v. - -iez
mang-é	il - -e, ils - -ent	il - -e-ait, ils - -e-aient, etc.

2) In Verbs ending in **-cer**, as: **tracer**, *to trace*, the **c** takes a *cedilla* whenever the inflection begins with **a** or **o**; as,

trac-er	je trac-e, n. traç-ons	je traç-ais, n. trac-ions
traç-ant	tu - -es, v. trac-ez	tu - -ais, v. - -iez
trac-é	il - -e, ils - -ent	il - -ait, ils traç-aient, etc.

Obs. to 1 and 2. The Final stem consonants **g** and **c** thus retain their soft pronunciation throughout the whole conjugation.

3) In Verbs ending in **-eler** and **-eter**, as **appeler**, *to call*, **jeter**, *to throw*, the **t** or **l** is doubled before an **e** mute: as,

appel-er	j' appell-e, n. appel-ons	appell-erai -erons	appell-erais, etc.
appel-ant	tu - -es, v. - -ez	- -eras -erez	
appel-é	il - -e, ils appell-ent	- -era -eront	

jet-er	je jett-e, n. jet-ons	jett-erai -erons	jett-erais, etc.
jet-ant	tu - -es, v. - -ez	- -eras -erez	
jet-é	il - -e, ils jett-ent	- -era -eront	

Exceptions: bourreler, celer, geler, harceler, peler; acheter, colleter, étiqueter, and their compounds, instead of doubling the consonant, take an accent grave over the e before l or t, as: il gèle, j'achète etc.

4) Verbs with an e mute or é in the Penultima, as: mener, *to lead*, céder, *to yield*, take a grave accent whenever the vowel of the following syllable is an e mute, (in the Fut. and Condit., however, é is retained): as,

men-er	je mèn-e,	n. men-ons	mèn-erai -erons	mèn-erais, etc.
men-ant	tu - -es,	v. - -ez	- -eras -erez	
men-é	il - -e,	ils mèn-ent	- -era -eront	

céd-er	je cèd-e,	n. céd-ons	but *Fut. & Condit.*	je céderai,
céd-ant	tu - -es,	v. - -ez	unchanged	je céderais, etc.
céd-é	il - -e,	ils cèd-ent		

Exceptions: Verbs ending -éger retain the é in all Tenses: as, protéger, *to protect*, je protége, etc.

5) Verbs ending in -ayer, -oyer, -uyer, change y into i before an e mute: as,

essayer, *to try*, j' essaie, nous essayons, j' essaierai, etc.
ployer, *to fold*, je ploie, nous ployons, je ploierai, etc.
essuyer, *to wipe*, j' essuie, nous essuyons, j' essuierai, etc.

Obs. 1. Those in -ayer, (also grasseyer) may be conjugated without changing y, as: je paye etc.

Obs. 2. Verbs in -ier are spelt with ii in the 1st and 2d Per. Pl. of the Imperf. Indic. and Pres^t. Subj., as: nous étudiions, vous priiez, etc.

---

6) Haïr (Old Germ. hatjan) *to hate*, retains the diæresis throughout except in the Sing. of the Pres^t. Indic. and Imperat.: as,

je hais, tu hais, il hait, *but*, nous haïssons, etc.

Obs. This is the only verb which does not take an accent circumflex in the 3^d P. Sing. Imperf. Subj.

7) Bénir (Lat. benedicere) *to bless*, has two forms for the Past Part.: béni, *fem.* bénie, *blessed;* and bénit, *fem.* bénite, *consecrated:* as, eau bénite.

8) Fleurir (Lat. floresco) in its literal sense *to blossom*, is always regular; but in the figurative sense *to be prosperous, to flourish*, it forms the Pres. Part. and Imperf. Indicat. thus: florissant, je florissais, etc.

B. PASSIVE VOICE.

INFINITIVE.

Pres. être aimé, *to be loved.*   *Past.* avoir été aimé, *to have been loved.*

PARTICIPLE.

Pres. étant aimé, *being loved.*   *Past.* ayant été aimé, *having been loved.*

INDICATIVE.

PRESENT.   P. INDEFINITE.

je	suis	aimé	(aimée)	*I am*	j'	ai	été aimé, *I have been*
tu	es	aimé	„	*[loved,*	tu	as	été aimé *[loved,*
il, on,	est	aimé			il, on,	a	été aimé
elle	est	aimée			elle	a	été aimée
nous	sommes	aimés	(aimées)		nous	avons	été aimés
vous	êtes	aimés	„		vous	avez	été aimés
ils	sont	aimés			ils	ont	été aimés
elles	sont	aimées.			elles	ont	été aimées.

IMPERFECT.   PLUPERFECT.

j' étais aimé, etc., *I was loved,*   j' avais été aimé, etc., *I had been*
nous étions aimés, etc.   nous avions été aimés, etc.   *[loved,*

PRETERITE.   ANTERIOR.

je fus aimé, etc., *I was loved,*   j' eus été aimé, etc., *I had been*
nous fûmes aimés, etc.   nous eûmes été aimés, etc.   *[loved,*

FUT. PRES.   FUTURE PAST.

je serai aimé, etc., *I shall be loved,*   j' aurai été aimé, etc., *I shall have*
nous serons aimés, etc.   nous aurons été aimés, etc. *[been loved,*

CONDITIONAL PRES.   CONDITIONAL PAST.

je serais aimé, etc., *I should be*   j' aurais été aimé, etc., *I should have*
nous serions aimés, etc.   *[loved,*   nous aurions été aimés, etc. *[been loved.*

IMPERATIVE.

soyons aimés, *let us be loved*
sois aimé, *be (thou) loved.*   soyez aimés, *be (ye) loved.*

SUBJUNCTIVE.

PRESENT.   PERFECT.

(que) je sois aimé, etc., *I may be*   (que) j' aie été aimé, etc., *I may have*
(que) n. soyons aimés, etc.   *[loved,*   (que) n. ayons été aimés, etc. *[been loved,*

IMPERFECT.   PLUPERFECT.

(que) je fusse aimé, *I might (should)*   (que) j' eusse été aimé, *I might*
be loved,   *(should) have been loved,*
(que) n. fussions aimés, etc.   (que) n. eussions été aimés, etc.

C. INTRANSITIVE VERBS (VERBES NEUTRES).

Intransitive Verbs are generally conjugated with **avoir**, except the following, which are conjugated with être:

aller	*to go*	éclore	*to be hatched, to blow*	retourner	*to return*
arriver	*to arrive*	entrer	*to enter*	sortir	*to go out*
décéder }	*to die*	naître	*to be born*	tomber	*to fall*
mourir }		partir	*to depart*	venir	*to come.*

Obs. 1. Two compounds of venir: **contrevenir à**, *to contravene*, **subvenir à**, *to relieve*, are conjugated with **avoir**.

Obs. 2. Whenever an intransitive Verb is used transitively, it must be conjugated with **avoir**, as,

Il a sorti le cheval de l'écurie; *He has brought the horse out of the stable.*

§ 87. Some Intransitive Verbs may be conjugated with **avoir** and **être**:

with **avoir** to denote the *action:*	with **être** to denote the *result* of the action, the actual *state* or *condition*.
La rivière a baissé aujourd'hui.	La rivière est bien baissée.
The river has fallen to-day.	*The river is very low.*

The following are the principal of these Verbs:

accourir	*to hasten*	déchoir	*to decay*	embellir	*to embellish*
apparaître	*to appear*	déborder	*to overflow*	empirer	*to grow worse*
disparaître	*to disappear*	monter	*to ascend*	grandir	*to grow*
baisser	*to sink*	descendre	*to descend*	rajeunir	*to grow young again*
changer	*to change*	échapper	*to escape*	rester	{ *to remain, (être)* / *to reside, (avoir)*
croître	{ *to grow,* / *to increase*	échouer	*to* { *strand* / *fail*	vieillir	*to grow old.*

D. REFLECTIVE VERBS (VERBES RÉFLÉCHIS.)

All Reflective Verbs are conjugated with être, *to be*, in the Compound Tenses.

INFINITIF.

Présent: se laver, *to wash one's self.* | *Passé*: s'être lavé, *to have washed one's self.*

PARTICIPE.

Présent: se lavant, *washing one's self.* | *Passé*: s'étant lavé, *having washed one's self.*

INDICATIF.

A. *Affirmatif.* PRÉSENT. B. *Négatif.*

Je	me	lave,	*I wash myself*	Je	ne me	lave	pas
tu	te	laves,	*thou washest thyself*	tu	ne te	laves	pas
il	se	lave,	*he washes himself*	il	ne se	lave	pas
on	se	lave,	*one washes one's self*	on	ne se	lave	pas
elle	se	lave,	*she washes herself*	elle	ne se	lave	pas
nous	nous	lavons,	*we wash ourselves*	nous	ne nous	lavons	pas
vous	vous	lavez,	*you wash yourselves*	vous	ne vous	lavez	pas
ils	se	lavent,	*they wash themselves*	ils	ne se	lavent	pas
elles	se	lavent,	*they wash themselves*	elles	ne se	lavent	pas

C. *Interrogatif.* D. *Négatif & Interrogatif.*

Me	lavé-je?*		Ne me	lavé-je pas?*
te	laves-tu?		ne te	laves-tu pas?
se	lave-t-il (-t-elle, -t-on?)		ne se	lave-t-il (-t-elle, -t-on) pas?
nous	lavons-nous?		ne nous	lavons-nous pas?
vous	lavez-vous?		ne vous	lavez-vous pas?
se	lavent-ils (-elles)?		ne se	lavent-ils pas?

IMPARFAIT. FUTUR PRÉSENT.

Je me lavais, *I was washing myself.* Je me laverai, *I shall wash myself.*

PRÉTÉRIT (DÉFINI.) CONDITIONNEL PRÉSENT.

Je me lavai, *I washed myself.* Je me laverais, *I should wash myself.*

IMPÉRATIF.

A. *Affirmatif.* B. *Négatif.*

lave-toi, *wash thyself* Ne te lave pas, *Do not wash thyself*
lavons-nous, *let us wash ourselves* ne nous lavons pas, *let us not wash ourselves*
lavez-vous, *wash yourselves* ne vous lavez pas, *do not wash yourselves.*

---

*or Est-ce que je me lave? etc.   Est-ce que je ne me lave pas? etc

PASSÉ INDÉFINI.

A. *I have washed (been washing) myself,* etc.

Je	me	suis lavé (ou lavée)
tu	t'	es lavé „
il	s'	est lavé
elle	s'	est lavée
on	s'	est lavé „
nous	nous	sommes lavés (ou lavées)
vous	vous	êtes lavés „
ils	se	sont lavés
elles	se	sont lavées

B. *I have not washed myself,* etc.

Je	ne me	suis	pas lavé (ou -e)
tu	ne t'	es	pas lavé „
il	ne s'	est	pas lavé
elle	ne s'	est	pas lavée
on	ne s'	est	pas lavé „
nous	ne nous sommes		pas lavés (ou -es)
vous	ne vous	êtes	pas lavés „
ils	ne se	sont	pas lavés
elles	ne se	sont	pas lavées

C. *Have I washed myself?* etc.

Me	suis-je	lavé (ou lavée)? *
t'	es-tu	lavé „ ?
s'	est-il (-elle)	lavé „ ?
nous	sommes-nous	lavés (ou lavées)?
vous	êtes-vous	lavés „ ?
se	sont-ils	lavés?
se	sont-elles	lavées?

*or Est-ce que je me suis lavé? etc.

D. *Have I not washed myself?*

Ne me	suis-je	pas lavé (ou -e)?*
ne t'	es-tu	pas lavé „ ?
ne s'	est-il (-elle)	pas lavé? „ ?
ne nous sommes-nous		pas lavés (ou -es)?
ne vous êtes-vous		pas lavés „ ?
ne se	sont-ils	pas lavés?
ne se	sont-elles	pas lavées?

Est-ce que je ne me suis pas lavé? etc.

PLUSQUEPARFAIT.

Je m'étais lavé, *I had washed myself.*

ANTÉRIEUR.

Je me fus lavé, *I had washed myself.*

FUTUR PASSÉ.

Je me serai lavé, *I shall have washed myself.*

CONDITIONNEL PASSÉ.

Je me serais lavé, *I should have washed myself.*

The Subjunctive is conjugated in the same manner:
Que je me lave (lavasse), etc.

Reciprocal Verbs are conjugated like Reflective Verbs: thus **Ils se trompent,** can signify *They deceive each other* or *themselves.* The ambiguity is avoided by adding **l'un l'autre, les uns les autres,** *one another* (§ 71 & 228).

READING LESSONS.

L'ARABE ET SON CHEVAL.

Les cavaliers du pacha d'Acre ayant recontré un Arabe et sa tribu qui s'en retournaient chargés de butin, fondirent sur eux à l'improviste, en tuèrent un grand nombre, firent les autres prisonniers, et, les ayant attachés avec des cordes, les emmenèrent à Acre pour en faire présent au pacha. L'Arabe ayant été grièvement blessé dans le combat, les Turcs l'avaient attaché sur un chameau et s'étaient emparés de son cheval qu'ils emmenaient également. Le soir du deuxième jour, ils campèrent avec leurs prisonniers dans les montagnes de Japhad; l'Arabe blessé avait les jambes liées ensemble par une courroie de cuir, et était étendu près de la tente où couchaient les Turcs. Pendant la nuit, tenu éveillé par la douleur de sa blessure, il entendit hennir son cheval parmi les autres chevaux attachés autour des tentes; il reconnut sa voix, et, ne pouvant résister au désir d'aller parler encore une fois à ce fidèle compagnon, il se traîna péniblement jusqu'à lui. "Pauvre ami, lui dit-il, que feras-tu parmi les Turcs? Ma femme et mes enfants ne t'apporteront plus le lait du chameau; ils ne te donneront plus l'orge dans le creux de la main; tu ne courras plus libre dans le désert, comme le vent d'Égypte; tu ne fendras plus du poitrail l'eau du Jouardain qui rafraîchissait ton poil aussi blanc que ton écume; qu'au moins, si je suis esclave, tu restes libre. Retourne à la tente que tu connais; va

dire à ma femme que ton maître ne reviendra plus, et passe la tête entre les rideaux de la tente pour lécher la main de mes petits enfants." En parlant ainsi, l'Arabe avait rongé avec ses dents la corde de poil de chèvre qui lui servait d'entraves, et l'animal était libre; mais, voyant son maître blessé et enchaîné à ses pieds, le fidèle et intelligent coursier comprit, avec son instinct, ce qu'aucune langue ne pouvait lui expliquer; il baissa la tête, flaira son maître, et, le saisissant avec les dents par la ceinture de cuir qu'il avait autour du corps, il partit au galop et l'emporta jusqu'à ses tentes. En arrivant et en jetant son maître sur le sable, aux pieds de sa femme et de ses enfants, le cheval expira de fatigue. Toute la tribu l'a pleuré; les poètes l'ont chanté, et son nom est constamment dans la bouche des Arabes de Jéricho.
A. de Lamartine.

MIEUX QUE ÇA.

L'empereur Joseph II n'aimait ni la représentation ni l'appareil, témoin ce fait qu'on se plaît à citer:

Un jour que, revêtu d'une simple redingote boutonnée, accompagné d'un seul domestique sans livrée, il était allé, dans une calèche à deux places qu'il conduisait lui-même, faire une promenade du matin aux environs de Vienne, il fut surpris par la pluie, comme il reprenait le chemin de la ville.

Il en était encore éloigné, lorsqu'un piéton, qui regagnait aussi la capitale, fait signe au conducteur d'arrêter: ce que Joseph II fait aussitôt. — Monsieur, lui dit le militaire (car c'était un sergent), y aurait-il de l'indiscrétion à vous demander une place à côté de vous? Cela ne vous gênerait pas prodigieusement, puisque vous êtes seul dans votre calèche, et ménagerait mon uniforme, que je mets aujourd'hui pour la première fois. — Ménageons votre uniforme, mon brave, lui dit Joseph, et mettez-vous là. D'où venez-vous? — Ah! dit le sergent, je viens de chez un garde-chasse de mes amis, où j'ai fait un fier déjeûner? — Qu'avez-vous donc mangé de si bon? — Devinez. — Que sais-je, moi... Une soupe à la bière? — Ah! bien oui, une soupe! mieux que ça. — De la choucroute? mieux que ça. — Une longe de veau? — Mieux que ça, vous dit-on. — Oh! ma foi! je ne puis deviner, dit Joseph. — Un faisan, mon digne homme, un faisan tiré sur les plaisirs de sa Majesté, dit le camarade en lui frappant sur la cuisse. — Tiré sur les plaisirs de Sa Majesté, il n'en devait être que meilleur. — Je vous en réponds.*

Comme on approchait de la ville, et que la pluie tombait toujours, Joseph demanda à son compagnon dans quel quartier il logeait, et où il voulait qu'on le descendît. — Monsieur, c'est trop de bonté, je craindrais d'abuser de... — Non, non, dit Joseph; votre rue? Le sergent, indiquant sa demeure, demanda à connaître celui dont il recevait tant d'honnêtetés. — A votre tour, dit Joseph, devinez. — Monsieur est militaire, sans doute? — Comme dit monsieur. — Lieutenant? — Ah! bien, oui, lieutenant; mieux que ça. — Capitaine? — Mieux que ça. — Colonel, peut-être? — Mieux que ça, vous dit-on. — Comment diable! dit l'autre en se rencognant aussitôt dans la calèche, seriez-vous feld-maréchal? — Mieux que ça. — Ah! mon Dieu, c'est l'Empereur! — Lui-même, dit Joseph, en montrant ses décorations. Il n'y avait pas moyen de tomber à genoux dans la voiture; l'invalide se confond en excuses et supplie l'Empereur d'arrêter pour qu'il puisse descendre. — Non pas, lui dit Joseph; après avoir mangé mon faisan, vous seriez trop heureux de vous débarrasser de moi aussi promptement; j'entends bien que vous ne me quittiez qu'à votre porte. — Et il l'y descendit.

*I should think so!   de Lévis.

LE PETIT PIERRE.

Je suis le petit Pierre
Du faubourg Saint-Marceau,
Messager ordinaire,
Facteur et porteur d'eau.
J'ai plus d'une ressource
Pour faire mon chemin :
Je n'emplis pas ma bourse,
Mais je gagne mon pain.

Je n'ai ni bois, ni terre,
Ni chevaux, ni laquais ;
Petit propriétaire,
Mon fonds est deux crochets.
Je prends comme il arrive
L'ivraie et le bon grain.
Dieu veut que chacun vive,
Et je gagne mon pain.

Contre un bel édifice
J'ai placé mon comptoir,
Là, sans parler au suisse,
Ou peut toujours me voir.
Pour n'oublier personne
Je me lève matin,
Et la journée est bonne
Quand je gagne mon pain.

Comme le disait Blaise,
Feu Blaise, mon parrain,
On est toujours à l'aise
Lorsque l'on n'a pas faim.
Dans les jours de misère,
Je m'adresse au voisin,
Il a pitié de Pierre,
Et je trouve mon pain.

Boucher de Perthes.

LE MONTAGNARD EMIGRÉ.

Combien j'ai douce souvenance
Du joli lieu de ma naissance !
Ma sœur, qu'ils étaient beaux ces jours
   De France !
O mon pays, sois mes amours
   Toujours.

Te souvient-il que notre mère
Au foyer de notre chaumière
Nous pressait sur son sein joyeux,
   Ma chère ?
Et nous baisions ses blonds cheveux
   Tous deux.

Ma sœur, te souvient-il encore
Du château que baignait la Dore,
Et de cette tant vieille tour
    Du More,
Où l'airain sonnait le retour
    Du jour?

Te souvient-il du lac tranquille
Qu'effleurait l'hirondelle agile,
Du vent qui courbait le roseau
    Mobile,
Et du soleil couchant sur l'eau
    Si beau?

Te souvient-il de cette amie,
Douce compagne de ma vie?
Dans le bois, en cueillant la fleur
    Jolie,
Hélène appuyait sur mon cœur
    Son cœur!

Oh! qui rendra mon Hélène,
Et ma montagne, et le grand chêne?
Leur souvenir fait tous les jours
    Ma peine:
Mon pays sera mes amours
    Toujours!
                    Châteaubriand.

LE RAT DE VILLE ET LE RAT DES CHAMPS.

Autrefois le rat de ville
Invita le rat des champs,
D'une façon fort civile,
A des reliefs d'Ortolans.

Sur un tapis de Turquie
Le couvert se trouva mis.
Je laisse à penser la vie
Que firent ces deux amis.

Le régal fut fort honnête,
Rien ne manquait au festin:
Mais quelqu'un troubla la fête
Pendant qu'ils étaient en train.

A la porte de la salle
Ils entendirent du bruit:
Le rat de ville détale;
Son camarade le suit.

Le bruit cesse, on se retire:
Rats en campagne aussitôt;
Et le citadin de dire:
„Achevons tout notre rôt."

„C'est assez, dit le rustique,
Demain vous viendrez chez moi.
Ce n'est pas que je me pique
De tous vos festins de roi:

Mais rien ne vient m'interrompre,
Je mange tout à loisir.
Adieu donc. Fi du plaisir
Que la crainte peut corrompre."

Lafontaine.

ENGLISH-FRENCH VOCABULARY.

A.

a, *un, une.*
to abandon, *abandonner.*
to abolish, *abolir.*
about, *environ.*
absent, *absent.*
to accompany, *accompagner.*
action, *action, f.*
to act, *agir.*
active, *actif.*
address, *adresse, f.*
admiral, *amiral.*
to admire, *admirer.*
advantage, *avantage, m.*
advice, *conseil, avis, m.*
to advise, *conseiller.*
affection, *amour, m., affection, f.*
Africa, *Afrique, f.*
afternoon, *après-midi, f.*
age, *âge, m.*
ago, *il y a.*
all, *tout, tous* (Ex. 97).
almost, *presque.*
aloud, *haut.*
Alps, *Alpes, f.*
already, *déjà.*
also, *aussi.*
altar, *autel, m.*
always, *toujours.*

ambassador, *ambassadeur.*
ambitious, *ambitieux.*
America, *Amérique, f.*
amiable, *aimable.*
among, *parmi.*
amusing, *amusant.*
ancient, *ancien.*
angry with, *fâché contre.*
to annoy, *ennuyer.*
another, *un autre.*
to answer, *répondre à.*
antiquity, *antiquité, f.*
Antwerp, *Anvers.*
any, Ex^s. 101, 121.
appetite, *appétit, m.*
to approve, *approuver.*
April, *avril, m.*
to arrive, *arriver.*
arm, *bras, m.*
army, *armée, f.*
as, *comme.*
ashamed, *honteux.*
to be ashamed, *avoir honte, f.*
Asia, *Asie, f.*
to ask, *demander.*
ass, *âne, m.*
assiduously, *assidûment.*
to assure, *assurer.*
at, *à.*
Athenian, *Athénien.*
Athens, *Athènes.*

to attack, *attaquer.*
August, *Août, m.*
aunt, *tante.*
Austria, *Autriche, f.*
Austrian, *autrichien.*
autumn, *automne, m.*
avarice, *avarice, f.*
awakened, *éveillé.*

B.

bad, *mauvais.*
badly, *mal.*
baker, *boulanger.*
banished, *banni.*
banner, *drapeau, m.*
bank, shore; *rive, f.*
banker, *banquier.*
barefoot, *nu-pieds* (Ex.109).
battle, *bataille, f.*
to beat, *battre, frapper.*
beautiful, *beau* (Ex. 107).
to be (in health), *se porter.*
because, *parce que.*
beer, *bière, f.*
before (time), *avant.*
- (place), *devant.*
- conj., *avant de.*
to beg, *demander, prier.*
to begin, *commencer.*
to behave, *se conduire.*
behaviour, *conduite, f.*
Belgium, *Belgique, f.*

ENGLISH-FRENCH VOCABULARY. 117

to believe, *croire.*
bell, *cloche, f.*
belong to, *sont à.*
belongs to, *est à.*
benefit, *bienfait, m.*
bent, *fléchi.*
to betray, *trahir.*
better (Ex. 91), *mieux.*
between, *entre.*
big, *grand.*
bird, *oiseau, m.*
bit, *morceau, m.*
bite, *mordre.*
black, *noir.*
to blame, *blâmer*
blessing, *bienfait, m.*
blue, *bleu.*
to blush, *rougir.*
boat, *bateau, m.*
bold, *hardi, téméraire.*
book, *livre, m.*
bookseller, *libraire.*
boot, *botte, f.*
to bore, *ennuyer.*
born, *né.*
bottle, *bouteille, f.*
bought, *acheté.*
box, *boîte, f.*
boy, *garçon, gamin.*
bread, *pain, m.*
breakfast, *déjeuner, m.*
bridge, *pont, m.*
brilliant, *brillant.*
to bring, *apporter.*
brother, *frère.*
brought, *apporté, amené.*
brown, *brun.*
Brussels, *Bruxelles.*
to build, *bâtir.*
bunch of grapes, *grappe (f.) de raisin, m.*
to burn, *brûler.*
to burst out, *éclater.*
but, *mais.*
but for, *sans.*
butter, *beurre, m.*
by, *par, en.*
by and by, *tantôt.*

C.

cake, *gâteau, m.*
to call, *appeler, nommer.*
can, *pouvoir.*
cape, *cap, m.*
capital, *capitale, f.*
captain, *capitaine.*
card, *carte, f.*
careless, *négligent.*
to carry off, *remporter.*
castle, *château, m.*
cat, *chat, m.*
cavalry, *cavalerie, f.*
cellar, *cave, f.*
certainly, *certainement.*
chair, *chaise, f.*
charming, *charmant.*
to chatter, *babiller.*
chemist, *pharmacien.*
cheerful, *gai.*
cherry, *cerise, f.*
to cherish, *chérir.*
child, *enfant, c.*
choose, *choisir.*
Christian, *chrétien.*
Christmas, *noël, m.*
church, *église, f.*
circumstance, *circonstan-*
citizen, *citoyen.* [*ce, f.*
class, *classe, f.*
clean, *propre.*
 - linen, *linge blanc.*
clear, *clair.*
to clear the table, *desservir.*
climate, *climat, m.*
cloak, *manteau, m.*
closed, *fermé.*
cloth, *drap, m.*
coat, *habit, m.*
cock, *coq.*
cold, *froid.*
it is cold, *il fait froid.*
colour, *couleur, f.*
come, p. p. *venu.*
come back, p. p. *revenu.*
 - down, p.p. *descendu.*
 - in, p. p. *entré.*

comfort, *consolation, f.*
to comfort, *consoler.*
to command, *commander.*
company, *compagnie, f., société, f.*
companion, *compagnon.*
to compare, *comparer.*
complexion, *teint, m.*
comprised, *compris.*
to conceive, *concevoir.*
conduct, *conduite, f.*
to confide, *confier.*
confidence, *confiance, f.*
to confound, *confondre.*
to congratulate, *féliciter.*
conqueror, *conquérant.*
conscience, *conscience, f.*
contented, *content.*
to continue, *continuer.*
contrary, *contraire.*
convinced, *convaincu.*
copper, *cuivre, m.*
copybook, *cahier, m.*
coral, *corail, m.*
corn, *blé, m.*
corner, *coin, m.*
corrected, *corrigé.*
cousin, *cousin, -e.*
counsel, *conseil, avis, m.*
count, *comte.*
country, *pays, m.*
 - (native), *patrie, f.*
 - (opp. to town), *campagne, f.*
country seat, *campagne, f.*
cover, *couverture, f.*
covered, *couvert.*
to cross, *franchir.*
crowd, *foule, f.*
cruel, *cruel.*
to cry, *crier.*
cup, *tasse, f.*
currant, *groseille, f.*

D.

danger, *danger, m.*
dark, *sombre, foncé.*

ENGLISH-FRENCH VOCABULARY.

daughter, *fille*.
day, *jour, m. journée, f.*
to-day, *aujourd'hui*.
to dance, *danser*.
dead, *mort*.
dear, *cher*.
death, *mort, f.*
decanter, *carafe, f.*
to deceive, *tromper*.
December, *décembre, m.*
to defeat, *battre*.
to defend, *défendre*.
delicious, *délicieux*.
delighted, *charmé*.
to deliver, *délivrer*.
to deny, *refuser*.
to depart, *partir*.
to despise, *mépriser*.
to descend, *descendre*.
desert, *désert, m.*
to deserve, *mériter*.
desk, *pupitre, m.*
detention, *retenue, f.*
dictation, *dictée, f.*
dictionary, *dictionnaire, m.*
difficult, *difficile*.
diligent, *appliqué*.
to dine, *dîner*.
dirty, *sale*.
disagreeable, *désagréable*.
disease, *maladie, f.*
disgraceful, *honteux*.
dismissed, *renvoyé*.
dispatch, *dépêche, f.*
dissatisfied, *mécontent*.
in the distance, *au lointain*.
distinctly, *distinctement*.
to disturb, *déranger*.
to do, *faire*.
dog, *chien, m.*
door, *porte, f.*
done, *fait*.
Dover, *Douvres*.
dozen, *douzaine, f.*
to draw, *dessiner*.
drawing, *dessin, m.*
drunk, *bu*.
dry, *sec* (Ex. 109).

during, *pendant*.
duty, *devoir, m.*

E.

ear, *oreille, f.*
earl, *comte*.
early, *tôt, de bonne heure*.
earth, *terre, f.*
Easter, *Pâques, m.*
easy, *facile*.
to eat, *manger*.
egg, *œuf, m.*
Egypt, *Égypte, f.*
ell, *aune, f.*
to embellish, *embellir*.
emperor, *empereur*.
empress, *impératrice*.
to empty, *vider*.
to endure, *supporter*
England, *Angleterre, f.*
English, *anglais*.
enemy, *ennemi, m.*
engraving, *estampe, f.*
to enjoy, *jouir de*.
to enter, *entrer*.
entertaining, *amusant*.
to entrust, *confier*.
envelope, *enveloppe, f.*
equal, *égal*.
essential, *essentiel*.
to establish, *établir*.
estate, *terre, f. domaine, m.*
to esteem, *estimer*.
even, (adv.) *même*.
event, *événement, m.*
evening, *soir, m.*
everybody, *tout le monde, chacun*.
evil, *mal, m.*
examination, *examen, m.*
to examine, *examiner*.
Exchange, *bourse, f.*
exercise, *exercice, thème, m.*
expected, *attendu*.
to expel, *chasser*.
expense, *dépense, f.*
expensive, *cher*.

experienced, *éprouvé*.
to explain, *expliquer*.
to expose, *exposer*.
eye, *œil, m.; pl. yeux*.
sore eyes, *mal aux yeux*.

F.

to fail, *manquer*.
fair (subst.) *foire, f.*
faith, *foi, f.*
faithful, *fidèle*.
false, *faux* (Ex. 109).
falsehood, *mensonge, m.*
to fall, *tomber*.
family, *famille, f.*
far, *loin*.
as far as, *jusqu'à*.
farmer, *fermier*.
fate, *sort, m.*
father, *père*.
fault, *faute, f.*
favourite, *favori* (Ex. 109).
favour, *faveur, f.*
fear, *crainte, f.*
feather, *plume, f.*
February, *février, m.*
fed, *nourri*.
to feel, *sentir*
fellow citizen, *concitoyen*.
to fetch, *aller chercher*.
fetters, *fers, m.*
few, *peu de* (Ex. 103).
to fill, *remplir*.
to find, *trouver*.
fine, *beau* (Ex. 107).
finger, *doigt, m.*
to finish, *finir*.
fire, *feu, m.*
first, *premier*.
fish, *poisson, m.*
fit, *propre*.
to fix, *fixer*.
flag, *pavillon, masc.*
to flatter, *flatter*.
fled, *fui*.
flower, *fleur, f.*
followed, *suivi*.

ENGLISH-FRENCH VOCABULARY. 119

following, *suivant.*
following day, *lendemain.*
foot, *pied, m.* [*m.*
for, prep. *pour.*
- conj. *car.*
to forbid, *défendre.*
foreigner, *étranger.*
forest, *forêt, f.*
to forget, *oublier.*
to forgive, *pardonner.*
fork, *fourchette, f.*
formerly, *autrefois.*
found, *trouvé.*
to found, *fonder.*
fought, *combattu.*
France, *France, f.*
Frederick, *Frédéric.*
to free, *affranchir, délivrer.*
French, *français.*
fresh, *frais* (Ex. 109).
friend, *ami, m., amie, f.*
friendship, *amitié, f.*
Friday, *vendredi, m.*
from, *de.*
fruit, *fruit, m.*
to fulfil, *remplir, accomplir.*

G.

game, play, *jeu, m.*
game, *gibier, m.*
garden, *jardin, m.*
gardener, *jardinier.*
gate, *porte, f.*
gathered, *cueilli.*
gay, *gai.*
general, *général.*
generous, *généreux.*
Geneva, *Genève.*
gentleman, *monsieur.*
gentlemanly, *commeilfaut*
geography, *géographie, f.*
German, *Allemand.*
Germany, *Allemagne, f.*
to give, *donner.*
to give back, *rendre.*
glass, *verre, m.*

glory, *gloire, f.*
glove, *gant, m.*
to go, *aller.*
to go in again, *rentrer.*
God, *Dieu.*
goddess, *déesse.*
gold, *or, m.*
gone out, *sorti.*
- back, *retourné.*
good, *bon, sage.*
gooseberry, *groseille* (*f.*)
à *maquerau.*
got, *obtenu.*
governess, *institutrice.*
government, *gouvernement, m.*
grain, *grain, m.*
grammar, *grammaire, f.*
grand-father, *grand-père,*
aieul.
grandmother, *grand'mère.*
grapes, *raisin, m.*
grass, *herbe, f.*
grateful, *reconnaissant.*
great, *grand.*
Great Britain, *Grande-Bretagne, f.*
Greece, *Grèce, f.*
Greek, *grec(-que).*
green, *vert.*
grief, *douleur, f., chagrin, m.*
to grieve, *attrister.*
to guard, *garder.*
Gustavus, *Gustave.*

H.

habit, *habitude, f.*
hair, *cheveu, m.*
half, *demi.*
ham, *jambon, m.*
hammer, *marteau, m.*
hand, *main, f.*
happy, *heureux.*
hard, *dur.*
hare, *lièvre, m.*
haughtiness, *orgueil, m.*

he who, *celui qui.*
head, *tête, f.*
head-ache, *mal à la tête.*
health, *santé, f.*
to hear, *entendre.*
heard, *entendu.*
heart, *cœur, m.*
heartily, *de bon cœur, de bon appetit.*
heaven, *ciel, m.; plur. cieux.*
heavy, *pesant.*
height, *hauteur, f.*
to help, *soutenir, aider.*
help, *secours, m., assistance, f.*
her (Ex. 115).
here, *ici.*
here is (are), *voici.*
hero, *héros.*
hers (Ex. 83).
high, *haut.*
hill, *colline, f.*
him (Ex. 115).
his (Ex. 83, 115).
history, *histoire, f.*
honey, *miel, m.*
holiday, *congé, m., vacances, f.*
at home (Ex. 151).
honest, *honnête.*
honest man, *homme de bien.*
to honour, *honorer.*
to hope, *espérer.*
horse, *cheval, m.*
hour, *heure, f.*
house, *maison, f.*
at the house of, *chez* (Ex. 151).
how, *comment.*
how far? } (Ex. 155).
- long? }
- many? } *combien.*
- much? }
human, *humain.*
hunger, *faim, f.*
to be hungry, avoir *faim.*

I.

I, *je, moi*, (Ex. 151).
ice, *glace, f.*
idea, *idée, f.*
idle, *paresseux.*
idleness, *paresse, f.*
if, *si.*
ill, *malade.*
illness, *maladie, f.*
to imitate, *imiter.*
immediately, *immédiatement.*
impressed, *imprimé.*
in, *en, dans.*
indeed, *en effet.*
industry, *assiduité, f.*
industrious, *industrieux, laborieux.*
in fact, *en effet.*
to inhabit, *habiter.*
inhabitant, *habitant.*
inhabited, *peuplé, habité.*
ink, *encre, f.*
inkstand, *encrier, m.*
instead of, *au lieu de.*
interesting, *intéressant.*
Ireland, *Irlande, f.*
Irish, *irlandais.*
iron, *fer, m.*
island, *île, f.*
itself, *se, soi.*
Italian, *italien.*
Italy, *Italie, f.*

J.

Jane, *Jeanne.*
James, *Jacques.*
January, *janvier, m.*
Jew, *juif.*
jewel, *bijou, m.*
John, *Jean.*
joined, *joint.*
joy, *joie, f.*
July, *juillet, m.*
June, *juin, m.*
just now, *tout à l'heure.*

K.

Kate, *Catherine.*
to keep, *conserver, garder.*
  - in, *enfermer.*
key, *clef, f.*
to kill, *tuer.*
kind, (subst.) *espèce, f.*
kindness, *bonté, f., complaisance, f.*
king, *roi.*
kingdom, *royaume, m.*
knee, *genou, m.*
knife, *couteau, m.*
to know, *connaître, savoir.*
known, *connu, su.*
knowledge, *connaissance, f.*

L.

lady, *dame, madame.*
young lady, *demoiselle, mademoiselle.*
lake, *lac.*
landing-place, *débarcadère, m.*
language, *langue, f.*
large, *grand.*
last, *dernier.*
last but one, *avant-dernier*
late, *tard.*
laundress, *blanchisseuse.*
lead, *plomb, m.*
lead-pencil, *crayon, m.*
leaf, *feuille, f.*
leap year, *année bissextile, f.*
to learn, *apprendre.*
learned, *appris, entendu.*
least, (Ex. 91, 93).
to leave, *quitter, laisser, partir.*
left, *laissé, parti.*
less, (Ex. 91) *moins.*
lesson, *leçon, f.*
letter, *lettre, f.*
librarian, *bibliothécaire.*
library, *bibliothèque.*

to lie (tell a lie), *mentir.*
life, *vie, f.*
to lift, *lever.*
to light, *allumer.*
like, *pareil, semblable.*
to be like, *ressembler.*
lion, *lion, m.*
to listen to, *écouter.*
little (adj.) *petit.*
  - (adv.) *peu de.*
loaded, *chargé.*
London, *Londres.*
long, *long, -ue.*
long ago, *depuis longtemps, il y a longtemps.*
a long time, *longtemps.*
to look at, *regarder.*
  - for, *chercher.*
to lose, *perdre.*
loss, *perte, f.*
at a loss, *à perte.*
lost, *perdu.*
love, *amour, m.*
to love, *aimer.*
low, *bas, -se.*
luggage, *bagage, m.*
lying, *mensonge, m.*

M.

mad, *enragé.*
made, *fait.*
maid servant, *servante.*
magnificent, *magnifique, superbe.*
to make, *faire.*
make, 3^d p. pl. *font.*
man, *homme.*
manners, *mœurs, f.*
many, *beaucoup de.*
so many, *tant de* (Ex.106).
March, *mars, m.*
to march, *marcher.*
mark, *marque, f., bon point, m.*
Mary, *Marie.*
master, *maître.*

ENGLISH-FRENCH VOCABULARY. 121

mathematics, *mathématiques, f.*
map, *carte, f.*
May, *mai, m.*
me, (Ex. 115, 125).
meadow, *prairie, f.*
means, *moyen, m.*
meanwhile, *cependant.*
meat, *viande, f.*
merchant, *négociant.*
to merit, *mériter.*
metal, *métal, m.*
midnight, *minuit.*
mine, (Ex. 83).
misfortune, *malheur, m.*
to miss, *manquer.*
Miss, *mademoiselle.*
to misuse, *abuser de.*
monarchy, *monarchie, f.*
Monday, *lundi, m.*
modesty, *modestie, f.*
money, *argent, m.*
month, *mois, m.*
monument, *monument, m.*
moon, *lune, f.*
more, *plus.*
morning, *matin, m.*
to-morrow, *demain.*
day after to-morrow, *après-demain.*
morsel, *morceau, m.*
Mrs., *madame.*
most (Ex. 93).
mother, *mère.*
mountain, *montagne, f.*
much, *beaucoup de* (Ex. 103).
how much, *combien de.*
too much, *trop de.*
so much, *tant de.*
so much the better, *tant mieux.*
museum, *musée, m.*
music, *musique, f.*
must, (Ex. 159).
mustard, *moutarde, f.*
my (Ex. 13).

N.

name, *nom, m.*
navy, *marine, f.*
near, *près de.*
nearly, *presque, à peu près.*
to need, *avoir besoin de.*
needle, *aiguille, f.*
neighbour, *voisin, -e.*
negro, *nègre.*
nephew, *neveu.*
new, *neuf, nouveau* (Ex. 107).
newspaper, *journal, m.*
niece, *nièce.*
night, *nuit, f.*
noise, *bruit, m.*
noisy, *bruyant.*
noon, *midi.*
not, *ne .. pas, ne .. point.*
not any, *ne .. point de.*
note, *billet, m.*
nothing, *ne .. rien.*
November, *novembre, m.*
now, *maintenant.*
nourished, *nourri.*
numerous, *nombreux.*
nursery maid, *bonne d'enfants.*
nut, *noix, f.*

O.

oar, *rame, f.*
to occupy, *occuper.*
October, *octobre, m.*
obedient, *obéissant.*
to obey, *obéir à.*
to be obliged, (Ex. 159).
to observe, *observer.*
obstinate, *obstiné.*
to obtain, *obtenir.*
of, *de.*
office, *bureau, m.*
officer, *officier.*
oil, *huile, f.*
old, *vieux,* (Ex.107) *ancien.*
on, *sur.*
at once, *tout de suite.*

one's self (Ex. 151) *soi.*
only, *ne .. que.*
open, opened, *ouvert.*
or, *ou.*
orange, *orange, f.*
order, *ordre, m.*
to order, *ordonner, commander, demander.*
orderly, *rangé, sage.*
ordinary, *ordinaire.*
ornament, *ornement, m.*
other, *autre.*
ours, (Ex. 83).
to owe, *devoir.*
owl, *hibou, m.*

P.

painter, *peintre.*
pair, *paire, f.*
patience, *patience, f.*
palace, *palais, m.*
pale, *pâle.*
pantry, *garde-manger, m.*
paper, *papier, m.*
parcel, *paquet, m.*
pardon, *pardon, m.*
parents, *parents, m.*
peace, *paix, f.*
pear, *poire, f.*
pebble, *caillou, m.*
pen, *plume, f.*
penknife, *canif, m.*
perceive, *apercevoir.*
perhaps, *peut-être.*
to permit, *permettre.*
Peter, *Pierre.*
physician, *médecin.*
piano, *piano, m.*
picture, *tableau, m.*
piece, *morceau, m.*
pin, *épingle, f.*
pity, *pitié, f.*
to pity, *plaindre.*
place, *place, f., rang,*
poste, *masc.*
placed, *mis.*
plain, *simple.*

plan, *plan, m.*
plant, *plante, f.*
plate, *assiette, f.*
to play, *jouer.*
to please, *plaire.*
pleasure, *plaisir, m. joie, f.*
pocket-book, *portefeuille, m.*
poem, *poème, m.*
poet, *poète.*
poetry, *poésie, f.*
poisonous, *vénéneux.*
Poland, *Pologne, f.*
polished, polite, *poli.*
politeness, *politesse, f.*
populous, *populeux.*
to possess, *posséder.*
possible, *possible.*
postage-stamp, *timbre-poste, m.*
postman, *facteur.*
post-office, *poste, f.*
pound, *livre, f.*
to pour out, *verser.*
powerful, *puissant.*
pray! *je vous en prie!*
to praise, *louer.*
precious, *précieux.*
to prefer, *préférer.*
to prepay, *affranchir.*
present, *cadeau, m.*
at present, *à présent.*
to preserve, *conserver.*
pretty, *joli.*
to prevent, *empêcher.*
price, *prix, m.*
pride, *orgueil, m.*
prince, *prince.*
princess, *princesse.*
printed, *imprimé.*
printing, *imprimerie, f.*
prize, *prix, m.*
prodigal, *prodigue.*
produces, *produit.*
product, *produit, m.*
profitable, *avantageux.*
project, *projet, m.*
to promise, *promettre.*

properly, *comme il faut.*
prudent, *prudent.*
Prussian, *Prussien.*
Prussia, *Prusse, f.*
public, *public* (Ex. 109).
to punish, *punir.*
purse, *bourse, f.*
pupil, *élève, c.; écolier.*
put, *mis.*
put off, *remis.*
put out of order, *dérangé.*
Pyrenees, *Pyrénées, f.*

Q.

quantity, *quantité, f.*
great quantity, *foule, f.*
queen, *reine.*
question, *question, f.*
quiet, *tranquille.*

R.

railway, *chemin de fer, m.*
  - station, *gare, f.*
to raise, *lever.*
raisins, *raisins secs, m.*
rank, *rang, m.*
rash, *imprudent.*
rather, *plutôt.*
to read, *lire,* p. p. *lu.*
ready, *prêt.*
reading, *lecture, f.*
really, *vraiment.*
reason, *raison, f.*
to receive, *recevoir.*
received, *reçu.*
reception, *accueil, m.*
recollection, *souvenir, m.*
red, *rouge.*
reed, *roseau, m.*
to reflect, *réfléchir.*
refreshment-room, *buffet,*
to refuse, *refuser.* [*m.*
relate, *raconter.*
relatives, *parents m.*
to render, *rendre,* p. p. *rendu.*

required, *nécessaire.*
all that is required, *tout ce qu'il faut.*
regiment, *régiment, m.*
to remain, *rester.*
remedy, *remède, m.*
to reply, *répondre.*
reproach, *reproche, m.*
republic, *république, f.*
to resemble, *ressembler.*
to reside, *demeurer.*
to retreat, *battre en retraite.*
to return, *retourner.*
revolution, *révolution, f.*
to reward, *récompenser.*
Rhine, *Rhin, m.*
rich, *riche.*
right, *droit.*
to be right, *avoir raison.*
to ring, *sonner.*
ripe, *mûr.*
road, *route, f.*
rock, *roc, rocher, m.*
Roman, *romain.*
roof, *toit, m.*
room, *chambre, f.*
rose, *rose, f.*
round, (adj.) *rond.*
  - (subj.) *tour, m.*
rule, *règle, f.*
Russia, *Russie, f.*

S.

sad, *triste.*
safe (subs.) *garde-manger, m.*
said, p. p. *dit.*
sail, *voile, f.*
same, *même.*
sand, *sable, m.*
satisfied, *satisfait, content.*
Saturday, *samedi, m.*
sausage, *saucisse, f.*
saving, *économie, f.*
to say, *dire.*
you say, *vous dites.*

ENGLISH-FRENCH VOCABULARY.

scholar, *écolier, savant.*
school, *école, f.*
Scotland, *Écosse, f.*
to search, *chercher.*
season, *saison, f.*
second, *second.*
seed, *grain, m.*
seen, *vu.*
to sell, *vendre.*
to send, *envoyer*
to send for, *envoyer chercher.*
to send back, *renvoyer.*
September, *septembre, m.*
seriously, *sérieusement.*
servant, *domestique, c.*
to serve, *servir.*
service, *service, m.*
to set out, *partir.*
severe, *sévère.*
several, *plusieurs.*
- times, *plusieurs fois.*
shame, *honte, f.*
for shame, *fi donc.*
shameful, *honteux.*
sheet (paper), *feuille, f.*
shepherd, *berger.*
ship, *vaisseau, m.*
shirt, *chemise, f.*
shoe, *soulier, m.*
shoemaker, *cordonnier, bottier.*
shop, *magazin, m.*
at the shop of, *chez.*
to show, *montrer.*
to shut, *fermer.*
to shut in, up, *enfermer.*
shy, *timide.*
sick, *malade.*
sideboard, *buffet, m.*
silence, *silence, m.*
similar, *semblable.*
sincere, *sincère.*
to sing, *chanter.*
Sir, *monsieur.*
sister, *sœur.*
situated, *situé.*
skill, *adresse, f.*

sky, *ciel, pl. cieux, m.*
slave, *esclave, c.*
to sleep, *dormir.*
slice, *tranche, f.*
small, *petit.*
snow, *neige, f.*
to snow, *neiger,*
so, *si, aussi, ainsi.*
society, *société, f.*
to soil, *salir.*
sold, *vendu.*
soldier, *soldat.*
some, (Ex. 101, 121).
son, *fils.*
song, *chanson, f.*
soon, *bientôt.*
as soon as, *aussitôt que.*
sooner, *plus tôt.*
sorry for, *fâché de.*
Spain, *Espagne, f.*
Spaniard, Spanish, *Espagnol.*
to speak, *parler.*
to spend, *dépenser.*
- (time) *passer.*
splendid, *splendide.*
spoken, *parlé.*
spoon, *cuiller, f.*
spot, *tache, f.*
spring, *printemps, m.*
star, *étoile, f.*
to start, *partir.*
to stay, *rester.*
steamboat, *bâteau à vapeur, m.*
steel, *acier, m.*
steel-pen, *plume métallique, f.*
stocking, *bas, m.*
storm, *tempête, f.*
to stop, *arrêter.*
stranger, *étranger.*
straw, *paille, f.*
strawberry, *fraise, f.*
street, *rue, f.*
strict, *sévère.*
to strike, *frapper.*
- (clock) *sonner.*

strong, *fort.*
student, *étudiant.*
studious, *studieux.*
to study, *étudier.*
study, *étude, f.*
to succeed in, *réussir à.*
succour, *secours, m.*
successor, *successeur.*
such, *tel, pareil.*
suffered, *souffert.*
sum, *somme, f.*
summer, *été, m.*
sun, *soleil, m.*
Sunday, *dimanche, m.*
supper, *souper, m.*
surprised, *surpris.*
sweet, *doux* (Ex. 109).
Switzerland, *Suisse, f.*

T.

table, *table, f.*
tailor, *tailleur.*
taken, *pris.*
to talk, *causer, babiller.*
tale, *conte, m.*
task, *devoir, m., tâche, f.*
- *pensum, m.*
taste, *goût, m.*
to taste, *goûter.*
tea, *thé, m.*
tell, *raconter, dire.*
- me, *dites-moi.*
term, *terme, m.*
to thank, *remercier*
than, *que.*
Thames, *Tamise, f.*
that (Ex. 145—148).
the (Exs. 1. 7. 23. 49).
theatre, *théâtre, m.*
thee (Ex. 115).
their, theirs (Ex. 83).
them (Ex. 115).
then, *alors* (time).
- *donc.*
there (Ex. 123), *là.*
- is (are), *voilà, il y a.*

these, (Ex. 23. 145).
thine, (Ex. 83).
to think, *penser à, songer à.*
thing, *chose, f.*
thirsty (to be) *avoir soif.*
this, those (Ex. 145).
Thursday, *jeudi, m.*
thus, *ainsi.*
thy, (Ex. 13).
ticket, *billet, m.*
time, *temps, m.*
- (multipl.) *fois, f.*
timid, *timide.*
tired, *las, fatigué.*
to, *à.*
tongue, *langue, f.*
too much, too many, *trop.*
tooth, *dent, f.*
tooth-ache, *mal aux dents.*
tower, *tour, f.*
town, *ville, f.*
tradesman, *marchand.*
train, *train, m.*
to translate, *traduire.*
translation, *traduction, version, f.*
travel, *voyage, m.*
to travel, *voyager.*
traveller, *voyageur.*
treasure, *trésor, m.*
tree, *arbre, m.*
tried, *éprouvé.*
trifle, *bagatelle, f.*
troops, *troupes, f.*
true, *vrai.*
truth, *vérité, f.*
twelve o'clock, *midi, minuit.*
turn, *tour, m.*
Tuesday, *mardi, m.*
tyrant, *tyran.*

U.

undertaking, *entreprise, f.*
ungratefulness, *ingratitude, f.*

umbrella, *parapluie, m.*
uncle, *oncle.*
under, *sous.*
to understand, *entendre, compendre.*
understood, *entendu, compris.*
unhappy, *malheureux.*
united, *uni.*
until, prep. *jusque.*
- conj. *jusqu'à ce que.*
unwell, *indisposé.*
upon, *sur.*
useful, *utile.*
useless, *inutile.*
usually, *ordinairement.*

V.

in vain, *en vain.*
to value, *estimer.*
vanity, *vanité, f.*
veil, *voile, m.*
very, *très, fort, bien.*
victorious, *victorieux.*
Vienna, *Vienne.*
village, *village, m.*
violin, *violon m.*
violent, *violent.*
virtuous, *vertueux.*
visit, *visite, f.*
to visit, *visiter.*

W.

waistcoat, *gilet, m.*
to wait, *attendre,* p. p. *attendu.*
walk, *promenade, f.*
to take a walk, *faire une promenade.*
to walk, *marcher.*
wall, *mur, m.*
want, *besoin, m.*
to want, *vouloir* (Ex. 155), *avoir besoin.*

war, *guerre, f.*
warrior, *guerrier.*
warm, *chaud.*
watch, *montre, f.*
water, *eau, f.*
way, *route, f., chemin, m.*
on the way, *chemin faisant.*
weather, *temps, m.*
Wednesday, *mercredi, m.*
week, *semaine, f.*
welcome, *accueil, m.*
well, *bien,* (Ex. 93).
wet, *mouillé.*
what, adj. *quel.*
- rel. pron. (Ex.147).
when, *quand, lorsque.*
whence, *d'où.*
where, *où.*
whether, *si.*
which, interrogat. *quel?*
- relative (Ex. 143).
while, *pendant que.*
white, *blanc,* (Ex. 109).
who, whom (Ex. 143).
why, *pourquoi.*
William, *Guillaume.*
willingly, *volontiers.*
wind, *vent, m.*
window, *fenêtre, f.*
wine, *vin, m.*
winter, *hiver, m.*
wise, *sage.*
to wish, *vouloir* (Ex. 157—159).
with, *avec.*
without, *sans.*
wood, *forêt, f.*
work, *ouvrage, m., œuvre, f., travail, m.*
to work, *travailler.*
world, *monde, m.*
worse, (Ex. 91, 93).
to worship, *adorer.*
worth, *valeur, f.*
is worth, *vaut.*
are worth, *valent.*
worthy, *digne.*

wretch, *misérable, m.*
to write, *écrire.*
written, *écrit.*
wrong, *injustice, f.,*
tort, m.
to be wrong, *avoir tort.*

Y.

year, *an, m.; année, f.*
yes, *oui.*
yesterday, *hier.*

yet, *cependant, encore.*
not yet, *pas encore.*
yoke, *joug, m.*
yonder, *là-bas.*
young, *jeune.*
yours, (Ex. 83).

VOCABULARY TO THE READING LESSONS.

L'Arabe et son cheval.

le cavalier, *horseman, the rider.*
rencontrer, *to meet.*
s'en retourner, *to return.*
le butin, *the booty.*
fondre, *to rush upon.*
à l'improviste, *unawares.*
tuer, *to kill.*
attacher, *to tie, bind.*
emmener, *to carry away.*
grièvement, *seriously.*
blesser, *to wound.*
s'emparer, *to seize.*
également, *equally, likewise.*
camper, *to encamp.*
la jambe, *the leg.*
lier, *to tie, fasten.*
ensemble, *together.*
la courroie, *the thong, the strap.*
le cuir, *the leather.*
étendre, *to stretch.*
coucher, *to lie.*
tenu, (P. P. of tenir) *held, kept.*
éveiller, *to awake.*
la blessure, *the wound.*
hennir, *to neigh.*
parmi, *among.*
autour de, *around.*
reconnut (Pret. of reconnaître), *recognized.*
la voix, *the voice.*
aller (allant, allé; Pres. je vais, tu vas, il va; Future: j'irai), *to go.*

encore une fois, *once more.*
se traîner, *to drag one's self.*
péniblement, *with difficulty.*
l'orge, f. *the barley.*
le creux, *the hollow.*
courir, *to run.*
libre, *free.*
le poitrail, *the chest.*
rafraîchir, *to refresh.*
le poil, *the hair.*
l'écume, f. *the foam, froth.*
au moins, *at least.*
connaître (connaissant, connu; je connais, je connus) *to know.*
va (see aller), *go.*
reviendra (Fut. of revenir), *will come back.*
le rideau, *the curtain.*
lécher, *to lick.*
ronger, *to gnaw.*
la chèvre, *the goat.*
servir de, *to serve for.*
l'entrave, f. *the fetter.*
voyant (Pres. Part. of voir, voyant, vu, je vois, je vis), *seeing.*
le coursier, *the steed.*
comprit (Pret. of comprendre, comprenant, compris), *understood.*
aucune, *no, no one.*
expliquer, *to explain.*
baisser, *to lower.*
flairer, *to smell, to scent.*
saisir, *to seize.*
la ceinture, *the girdle, belt.*

le corps, *the body.*
emporter, *to carry of.*
jeter, *to throw.*
pleurer, *to weep, lament.*
constamment, *constantly.*
la bouche, *the mouth.*

Mieux que ça.

ça, (contraction of cela), *that.*
la représentation, *the display.*
l'appareil, *the show.*
témoin, *witness.*
le fait, *the fact.*
se plaire, *to take pleasure.*
citer, *to quote.*
revêtir, *to dress.*
la redingote, *the frock coat.*
boutonner, *to button.*
la calèche, *the carriage.*
conduire, *to lead, drive.*
faire une promenade, *to take a walk.*
la pluie, *the rain.*
reprendre, *to resume, retrace.*
le chemin, *the way, road.*
éloigné, *far, distant.*
le piéton, *the pedestrian.*
regagner, *to return to.*
le conducteur, *the driver.*
le côté, *the side.*
gêner, *to inconvenience.*
seul, *alone.*
ménager, *to save.*
mettre, *to put on.*
se mettre, *to place one's self.*

venir (venant, venu, je viens) *to come.*
le garde-chasse, *the gamekeeper.*
fier, (lit. *proud*) *rare.*
deviner, *to guess.*
je sais, (Pres. of **savoir**, sachant, su; je sais, je sus, saurai), *I know.*
la choucroute, *sourkrout.*
la longe, *the loin.*
le veau, *the calf, veal.*
puis (from **pouvoir**), *I can.*
la foi, *the faith.*
le faisan, *the pheasant.*
tirer, *to shoot.*
la cuisse, *the thigh, leg.*
devoir, *to owe, must.*
répondre de, *to answer for.*
craindre, *to fear.*
la rue, *the street.*
le demeure, *the residence.*
l'honnêteté, *the politeness.*
le tour, *the turn.*
se rencogner, *to put one's self in the corner.*
montrer, *to show.*
le moyen, *the means.*
le genou, *the knee.*
se confondre en, *to be profuse in.*
supplier, *to entreat.*
pour que (with the Subj.) *in order that.*
puisse (Pres. Subj. of **pouvoir**), *may.*
se débarrasser, *to get rid of.*
promptement, *quickly.*
entendre, *to hear, to mean.*
descendre (trans.) *to set down.*

Le Petit Pierre.

le faubourg, *the suburb.*
le messager, *the messenger.*

le facteur, *the letter-carrier*
le porteur, *the carrier.*
emplir, *to fill.*
gagner, *to earn.*
ni...ni, *neither...nor.*
la terre, *the estate.*
le propriétaire, *the proprietor.*
le fonds, *the funds, capital.*
le crochet, *the hook, the porter's knot.*
l'ivraie, *the weed.*
veut (Pres. of **vouloir**, Ex. 157), *wishes.*
chacun, *every body.*
vivre, *to live.*
contre, *against.*
le comptoir, *the counter.*
le suisse, *the porter.*
oublier, *to forget.*
la journée, *the day's work.*
disait (Imp. of **dire**), *said.*
feu, *deceased, late.*
le parrain, *the godfather.*
à l'aise, *comfortable.*

Le Montagnard émigré.

la souvenance, (poetical) *the remembrance.*
la naissance, *the birth.*
il te souvient, *you remember.*
le foyer, *the hearth.*
la chaumière, *the cottage.*
le sein, *the bosom.*
baiser, *to kiss.*
baigner, *to bathe.*
la Dore, *a river in France.*
le More, *the Moor.*
l'airain, (lit. *brass*) *bell.*
effleurer, *to graze, touch slightly.*
l'hirondelle, *the swallow.*
agile, *swift.*
courber, *to bend.*
le roseau, *the reed.*

mobile, *moveable, shaking.*
couchant, *setting.*
cueillir, *to gather.*
appuyer, *to lean.*
le chêne, *the oak.*
le souvenir, *the remembrance.*
la peine, *the grief.*

Le rat de ville et le rat des champs.

autrefois, *formerly, once upon a time.*
la façon, *the fashion, way.*
reliefs, *scraps.*
l'ortolan, *ortolan (a little bird).*
le tapis, *the carpet.*
le couvert, *the cover, cloth.*
laisser à penser, *to leave to imagine.*
firent (Pres. of **faire**), *led.*
régal, *the treat.*
honnête, *decent.*
manquer à, *to be wanting.*
le festin, *the feast.*
troubler, *to disturb.*
pendant que, *whilst.*
en train, *at it.*
la salle, *the hall.*
détaler, *to make off.*
suit (Pres. of **suivre**), *follows.*
cesser, *to cease.*
en campagne, *at work.*
le citadin, *the citizen.*
de dire, *began to say.*
achever, *to finish.*
le rôt, *the roast meat.*
chez moi (Ex. 151), *to (at) my home.*
interrompre, *to interrupt.*
à loisir, *at leisure.*
adieu, *farewell.*
fi de..., *out upon.*
corrompre, *to spoil.*

BOOKS FOR THE STUDY

OF THE

FRENCH LANGUAGE.

PUBLISHED BY

WILLIAMS AND NORGATE.

Crown 8vo. Cloth, price 2s each.

The Student's Graduated French Reader, for the use of Public Schools. By LEON DELBOS, M.A., of King's College, London. I. First Year. Anecdotes, Tales, Historical Pieces. Edited with Notes and a Complete Vocabulary. 2nd Edition.

The Student's Graduated French Reader, for the use of Public Schools. II. Second Year. Historical Pieces and Tales. 180 pp. 2nd Edition.

"It would be no easy matter to find a second French Reader more completely satisfactory in every respect than that of M. Delbos. The contents which have been selected with great care and judgment, from authors of the highest standing, consist of portions of history, biography, anecdotes and fiction, full of interest and written in the purest French. . . The arrangements of the materials is no less happy than their selection, the shorter extracts being often grouped under general heads, and carefully graduated in difficulty. . . .The explanatory notes here and there, and the Index at the end, will be found of great use."—*Athenæum.*

" Very well selected."—*Saturday Review.*

"A better book will always supplant those that are inferior. . . The intrinsic merits of this series justify their appearance. . . The extracts are well chosen with a view to interest the translator."—*Educational Times.*

" The utility of the book is enhanced by numerous notes and a vocabulary."—*Scotsman.*

" This is a very satisfactory collection from the best authors, selected with great care and supplied with adequate notes. . . . A thoroughly good book of this kind should in fact be calculated to inspire a taste for literature in the student's mind. The volumes edited by M. Delbos fairly meet this requirement."

"The notes are critical and explanatory. The book is well printed and excellently got up."—*Educational Times.*

"They are, without exception, good examples of classic French, and both on that account and from their intrinsic literary merits are well fitted for class study. . . . A number of useful notes."—*Scotsman.*

Crown 8vo. Cloth, 1s 6d each.

French Classics for English Students. Edited, with Introduction and Notes, by LEON DELBOS, M.A., of King's College.

1. Racine. Les Plaideurs. 1s 6d.
2. Corneille. Horace. 1s 6d.
3. Corneille. Cinna. 1s 6d.
4. Molière. Le Bourgeois Gentilhomme. 1s 6d.
5. Corneille. Le Cid. 1s 6d.
6. Molière. Les Précieuses Ridicules. 1s 6d.
7. Chateaubriand. Voyage en Amérique. 1s 6d.
8. Xav. de Maistre. Prisonniers du Caucase and Le Preux d'Aoste. 1s 6d.
9. Lafontaine's Fables. 1s 6d.

"Compared with other books having the same aim, these books deserve very favourable mention. For the notes are well selected; they never commit the capital fault of trespassing on the province of the grammar or the dictionary, and so pandering to the pupil's laziness, and they are, moreover, generally well expressed and to the point."—*Saturday Review.*

"Carefully edited, and is prefaced by a useful and interesting account of the life and writings of the author."—*Educational Times.*

French for Beginners. Lessons Systematic, Practical, and Etymological. By J. LEMAISTRE. To precede Eugène's Method and the various Elementary French Books. *Cloth* 2s 6d

Colloquial French, for School and Private Use. By H. TARVER. B.-ès-L., late of Eton College. 328 pp. Crown 8vo. *Cloth* 5s

Delbos (Prof. Leon) THE STUDENT'S FRENCH COMPOSITION, on an entirely new plan. With Introduction and Notes. Crown 8vo. *Cloth* 3s 6d

Little Eugene's French Reader. For Beginners. Anecdotes and Tales. Edited, with Notes and a complete Vocabulary, by LEON DELBOS, M.A., of King's College. Crown 8vo. *Cloth* 2s 6d

Victor Hugo. NOTRE DAME DE PARIS. Adopted for the use of Schools and Colleges. By J. BOÏELLE, B.A., Senior French Master, Dulwich College. 2 vols. Crown 8vo. *Cloth* 3s each

Victor Hugo. LES MISÉRABLES. Les Principaux Épisodes. Edited, with Life and Notes, by J. BOÏELLE, Senior French Master, Dulwich College. 2 vols. Crown 8vo. 3s 6d each

La Roche-Jaquelin. SCENES FROM THE WAR IN LA VENDÉE. Edited, with Notes, by C. SCUDAMORE, M.A. With a Map. Crown 8vo. *Cloth* 2s

Foa (Mad. Eugen.) CONTES HISTORIQUES, with idiomatic Notes by G. A. NEVEU. Second Edition. *Cloth* 2s

Krueger (H.) FRENCH GRAMMAR. 5th Edition. 12mo. *Cloth* 1s

Delbos (L.) FRENCH ACCIDENCE AND MINOR SYNTAX. Crown 8vo. 2nd Edition. *Cloth* 1s 6d

14, Henrietta Street, Covent Garden, London; and
20, South Frederick Street, Edinburgh.

WILLIAMS AND NORGATE'S
LIST OF
French, German, Italian, Latin and Greek,
AND OTHER
SCHOOL BOOKS AND MAPS.

French.

FOR PUBLIC SCHOOLS WHERE LATIN IS TAUGHT.

Eugène (G.) The Student's Comparative Grammar of the French Language, with an Historical Sketch of the Formation of French. For the use of Public Schools. With Exercises. By G. Eugène-Fasnacht, French Master, Westminster School. 11th Edition, thoroughly revised. Square crown 8vo, cloth. 5s.

Or Grammar, 3s.; Exercises, 2s. 6d.

"The appearance of a Grammar like this is in itself a sign that great advance is being made in the teaching of modern languages..... The rules and observations are all scientifically classified and explained."—*Educational Times.*

"In itself this is in many ways the most satisfactory Grammar for beginners that we have as yet seen."—*Athenæum.*

Eugène's French Method. Elementary French Lessons. Easy Rules and Exercises preparatory to the "Student's Comparative French Grammar." By the same Author. 9th Edition. Crown 8vo, cloth. 1s. 6d.

"Certainly deserves to rank among the best of our Elementary French Exercise-books."—*Educational Times.*

Delbos. Student's Graduated French Reader, for the use of Public Schools. I. First Year. Anecdotes, Tales, Historical Pieces. Edited, with Notes and a complete Vocabulary, by Leon Delbos, M.A., of King's College, London. 3rd Edition. Crown 8vo, cloth. 2s.

——— The same. II. Historical Pieces and Tales. 3rd Edition. Crown 8vo, cloth. 2s.

Little Eugène's French Reader. For Beginners. Anecdotes and Tales. Edited, with Notes and a complete Vocabulary, by Leon Delbos, M.A., of King's College. 2nd Edition. Crown 8vo, cloth. 1s. 6d.

Krueger (H.) Short French Grammar. 6th Edition. 180 pp. 12mo, cloth. 2s.

Victor Hugo. Les Misérables, les principaux Episodes. With Life and Notes by J. Boïelle, Senior French Master, Dulwich College. 2 vols. Crown 8vo, cloth. Each 3s. 6d.

——— Notre-Dame de Paris. Adapted for the use of Schools and Colleges, by J. Boïelle, B.A., Senior French Master, Dulwich College. 2 vols. Crown 8vo, cloth. Each 3s.

Boïelle. French Composition through Lord Macaulay's English. I. Frederic the Great. Edited, with Notes, Hints, and Introduction, by James Boïelle, B.A. (Univ. Gall.), Senior French Master, Dulwich College, &c. &c. Crown 8vo, cloth. 3s.

Foa (Mad. Eugen.) Contes Historiques. With Idiomatic Notes by G. A. Neveu. 3rd Edition. Crown 8vo, cloth. 2s.

Larochejacquelein (Madame de) Scenes from the War in the Vendée. Edited from her Mémoirs in French, with Introduction and Notes, by C. Scudamore, M.A. Oxon, Assistant Master, Forest School, Walthamstow. Crown 8vo, cloth. 2s.

French Classics for English Schools. Edited, with Introduction and Notes, by Leon Delbos, M.A., of King's College. Crown 8vo, cloth.

No. 1. Racine's Les Plaideurs. 1s. 6d.
No. 2. Corneille's Horace. 1s. 6d.
No. 3. Corneille's Cinna. 1s. 6d.
No. 4. Molière's Bourgeois Gentilhomme. 1s. 6d.
No. 5. Corneille's Le Cid. 1s. 6d.
No. 6. Molière's Précieuses Ridicules. 1s. 6d.
No. 7. Chateaubriand's Voyage en Amérique. 1s. 6d.
No. 8. De Maistre's Prisonniers du Caucase and Lepreux d'Aoste. 1s. 6d.
No. 9. Lafontaine's Fables Choisies. 1s. 6d.

Lemaistre (J.) French for Beginners. Lessons Systematic, Practical and Etymological. By J. Lemaistre. Crown 8vo, cloth. 2s. 6d.

Roget (F. F.) Introduction to Old French. History, Grammar, Chrestomathy, Glossary. 400 pp. Crown 8vo, cl. 6s.

Foreign School Books and Maps. 3

Kitchin. Introduction to the Study of Provençal. By Darcy B. Kitchin, B.A. [Literature—Grammar—Texts—Glossary.] Crown 8vo, cloth. 4s. 6d.

Tarver. Colloquial French, for School and Private Use. By H. Tarver, B.-ès-L., late of Eton College. 328 pp., crown 8vo, cloth. 5s.

Ahn's French Vocabulary and Dialogues. 2nd Edition. Crown 8vo, cloth. 1s. 6d.

Delbos (L.) French Accidence and Minor Syntax. 2nd Edition. Crown 8vo, cloth. 1s. 6d.

—— Student's French Composition, for the use of Public Schools, on an entirely new Plan. 250 pp. Crown 8vo, cloth. 3s. 6d.

Vinet (A.) Chrestomathie Française ou Choix de Morceaux tirés des meilleurs Ecrivains Français. 11th Edition. 358 pp., cloth. 3s. 6d.

Roussy. Cours de Versions. Pieces for Translation into French. With Notes. Crown 8vo. 2s. 6d.

Williams (T. S.) and J. Lafont. French Commercial Correspondence. A Collection of Modern Mercantile Letters in French and English, with their translation on opposite pages. 2nd Edition. 12mo, cloth. 4s. 6d.

For a German Version of the same Letters, vide p. 4.

Fleury's Histoire de France, racontée à la Jeunesse, with Grammatical Notes, by Auguste Beljame, Bachelier-ès-lettres. 3rd Edition. 12mo, cloth boards. 3s. 6d.

Mandrou (A.) French Poetry for English Schools. Album Poétique de la Jeunesse. By A. Mandrou, M.A. de l'Académie de Paris. 2nd Edition. 12mo, cloth. 2s.

German.

Schlutter's German Class Book. A Course of Instruction based on Becker's System, and so arranged as to exhibit the Self-development of the Language, and its Affinities with the English. By Fr. Schlutter, Royal Military Academy, Woolwich. 5th Edition. 12mo, cloth. (Key, 5s.) 5s.

Möller (A.) A German Reading Book. A Companion to SCHLUT-
TER'S German Class Book. With a complete Vocabulary.
150 pp. 12mo, cloth. 2s.

Ravensberg (A. v.) Practical Grammar of the German Language.
Conversational Exercises, Dialogues and Idiomatic Ex-
pressions. 3rd Edition. Cloth. (Key, 2s.) 5s.

—————— **English into German.** A Selection of Anecdotes,
Stories, &c., with Notes for Translation. Cloth. (Key,
5s.) 4s. 6d.

—————— **German Reader,** Prose and Poetry, with copious Notes
for Beginners. 2nd Edition. Crown 8vo, cloth. 3s.

Weisse's Complete Practical Grammar of the German Language,
with Exercises in Conversations, Letters, Poems and
Treatises, &c. 4th Edition, very much enlarged and
improved. 12mo, cloth. 6s.

—————— **New Conversational Exercises** in German Composition,
with complete Rules and Directions, with full Refer-
ences to his German Grammar. 2nd Edition. 12mo,
cloth. (Key, 5s.) 3s. 6d.

Wittich's German Tales for Beginners, arranged in Progressive
Order. 26th Edition. Crown 8vo, cloth. 4s.

—————— **German for Beginners,** or Progressive German Exercises. 8th Edition. 12mo, cloth. (Key, 5s.) 4s.

—————— **German Grammar.** 10th Edition. 12mo, cloth. 4s. 6d.

Hein. German Examination Papers. Comprising a complete
Set of German Papers set at the Local Examinations in
the four Universities of Scotland. By G. Hein, Aberdeen
Grammar School. Crown 8vo, cloth. 2s. 6d.

Schinzel (E.) Child's First German Course; also, A Complete
Treatise on German Pronunciation and Reading. Crown
8vo, cloth. 2s. 6d.

—————— **German Preparatory Course.** 12mo, cloth. 2s. 6d.

—————— **Method of Learning German.** (A Sequel to the Preparatory Course.) 12mo, cloth. 3s. 6d.

Apel's Short and Practical German Grammar for Beginners, with
copious Examples and Exercises. 3rd Edition. 12mo,
cloth. 2s. 6d.

Sonnenschein and Stallybrass. German for the English. Part I.
First Reading Book. Easy Poems with interlinear Trans-
lations, and illustrated by Notes and Tables, chiefly
Etymological. 4th Edition. 12mo, cloth. 4s. 6d.

Williams (T. S.) Modern German and English Conversations and Elementary Phrases, the German revised and corrected by A. Kokemueller. 21st enlarged and improved Edition. 12mo, cloth. 3s. 6d.

——— and C. Cruse. German and English Commercial Correspondence. A Collection of Modern Mercantile Letters in German and English, with their Translation on opposite pages. 2nd Edition. 12mo, cloth. 4s. 6d.

For a French Version of the same Letters, vide p. 2.

Apel (H.) German Prose Stories for Beginners (including Lessing's Prose Fables), with an interlinear Translation in the natural order of Construction. 12mo, cloth. 2s. 6d.

——— German Prose. A Collection of the best Specimens of German Prose, chiefly from Modern Authors. 500 pp. Crown 8vo, cloth. 3s.

German Classics for English Students. With Notes and Vocabulary. Crown 8vo, cloth.

Schiller's Lied von der Glocke (the Song of the Bell), and other Poems and Ballads. By M. Förster. 2s.
——— Maria Stuart. By M. Förster. 2s. 6d.
——— Minor Poems and Ballads. By Arthur P. Vernon. 2s.
Goethe's Iphigenie auf Tauris. By H. Attwell. 2s.
——— Hermann und Dorothea. By M. Förster. 2s. 6d.
——— Egmont. By H. Apel. 2s. 6d.
Lessing's Emilia Galotti. By G. Hein. 2s.
——— Minna von Barnhelm. By J. A. F. Schmidt. 2s. 6d.
Chamisso's Peter Schlemihl. By M. Förster. 2s.
Andersen's Bilderbuch ohne Bilder. By Alphons Beck. 2s.
Nieritz. Die Waise, a German Tale. By E. C. Otte. 2s. 6d.
Hauff's Mærchen. A Selection. By A. Hoare. 3s. 6d.

Carové (J. W.) Mærchen ohne Ende (The Story without an End). 12mo, cloth. 2s.

Fouque's Undine, Sintram, Aslauga's Ritter, die beiden Hauptleute. 4 vols. in 1. 8vo, cloth. 7s. 6d.

Undine. 1s. 6d.; cloth, 2s.   Aslauga. 1s. 6d.; cloth, 2s.
Sintram. 2s. 6d.; cloth, 3s.   Hauptleute. 1s. 6d.; cloth, 2s.

Latin and Greek.

Cæsar de Bello Gallico. Lib. I. Edited, with Introduction, Notes and Maps, by Alexander M. Bell, M.A., Ball. Coll. Oxon. Crown 8vo, cloth. 2s. 6d.

Euripides' Medea. The Greek Text, with Introduction and Explanatory Notes for Schools, by J. H. Hogan. 8vo, cloth. 3s. 6d.

—— **Ion.** Greek Text, with Notes for Beginners, Introduction and Questions for Examination, by Dr. Charles Badham, D.D. 2nd Edition. 8vo. 3s. 6d.

Æschylus. Agamemnon. Revised Greek Text, with literal line-for-line Translation on opposite pages, by John F. Davies, B.A. 8vo, cloth. 3s.

Platonis Philebus. With Introduction and Notes by Dr. C. Badham. 2nd Edition, considerably augmented. 8vo, cloth. 4s.

—— **Euthydemus et Laches.** With Critical Notes and an Epistola critica to the Senate of the Leyden University, by Dr. Ch. Badham, D.D. 8vo, cloth. 4s.

—— **Symposium,** and Letter to the Master of Trinity, "De Platonis Legibus,"—Platonis Convivium, cum Epistola ad Thompsonum edidit Carolus Badham. 8vo, cloth. 4s.

Sophocles. Electra. The Greek Text critically revised, with the aid of MSS. newly collated and explained. By Rev. H. F. M. Blaydes, M.A., formerly Student of Christ Church, Oxford. 8vo, cloth. 6s.

—— **Philoctetes.** Edited by the same. 8vo, cloth. 6s.

—— **Trachiniæ.** Edited by the same. 8vo, cloth. 6s.

—— **Ajax.** Edited by the same. 8vo, cloth. 6s.

Dr. D. Zompolides. A Course of Modern Greek, or the Greek Language of the Present Day. I. The Elementary Method. Crown 8vo. 5s.

Kiepert's New Atlas Antiquus. Maps of the Ancient World, for Schools and Colleges. 6th Edition. With a complete Geographical Index. Folio, boards. 7s. 6d.

Kampen. 15 Maps to illustrate Cæsar's De Bello Gallico. 15 coloured Maps. 4to, cloth. 3s. 6d.

Italian.

Volpe (Cav. G.) Eton Italian Grammar, for the use of Eton College. Including Exercises and Examples. New Edition. Crown 8vo, cloth. 4s. 6d.
———— Key to the Exercises. 1s.
Rossetti. Exercises for securing Idiomatic Italian by means of Literal Translations from the English, by Maria F. Rossetti. 12mo, cloth. 3s. 6d.
———— Aneddoti Italiani. One Hundred Italian Anecdotes, selected from "Il Compagno del Passeggio." Being also a Key to Rossetti's Exercises. 12mo, cloth. 2s. 6d.
Venosta (F.) Raccolta di Poesie tratti dai piu celebri autori antichi e moderni. Crown 8vo, cloth. 5s.
Christison (G.) Racconti Istorici e Novelle Morali. Edited for the use of Italian Students. 12th Edition. 18mo, cloth. 1s. 6d.

Danish—Dutch.

Bojesen (Mad. Marie) The Danish Speaker. Pronunciation of the Danish Language, Vocabulary, Dialogues and Idioms for the use of Students and Travellers in Denmark and Norway. 12mo, cloth. 4s.
Williams and Ludolph. Dutch and English Dialogues, and Elementary Phrases. 12mo. 2s. 6d.

Wall Maps.

Sydow's Wall Maps of Physical Geography for School-rooms, representing the purely physical proportions of the Globe, drawn in a bold manner. An English Edition, the Originals with English Names and Explanations. Mounted on canvas, with rollers :

1. The World. 2. Europe. 3. Asia. 4. Africa. 5. America (North and South). 6. Australia and Australasia.
Each 10s.
———— Handbook to the Series of Large Physical Maps for School Instruction, edited by J. Tilleard. 8vo. 1s.

Miscellaneous.

De Rheims (H.). Practical Lines in Geometrical Drawing, containing the Use of Mathematical Instruments and the Construction of Scales, the Elements of Practical and Descriptive Geometry, Orthographic and Horizontal Projections, Isometrical Drawing and Perspective. Illustrated with 300 Diagrams, and giving (by analogy) the solution of every Question proposed at the Competitive Examinations for the Army. 8vo, cloth. 9s.

Fyfe (W. T.) First Lessons in Rhetoric. With Exercises. By W. T. Fyfe, M.A., Senior English Master, High School for Girls, Aberdeen. 12mo, sewed. 1s.

Fuerst's Hebrew Lexicon, by Davidson. A Hebrew and Chaldee Lexicon to the Old Testament, by Dr. Julius Fuerst. 5th Edition, improved and enlarged, containing a Grammatical and Analytical Appendix. Translated by Rev. Dr. Samuel Davidson. 1600 pp., royal 8vo, cloth. 21s.

Strack (W.) Hebrew Grammar. With Exercises, Paradigms, Chrestomathy and Glossary. By Professor H. Strack, D.D., of Berlin. Crown 8vo, cloth. 4s. 6d.

Hebrew Texts. Large type. 16mo, cloth.
    Genesis. 1s. 6d. Psalms. 1s. Job. 1s. Isaiah. 1s.

Turpie (Rev. Dr.) Manual of the Chaldee Language: containing Grammar of the Biblical Chaldee and of the Targums, and a Chrestomathy, consisting of Selections from the Targums, with a Vocabulary adapted to the Chrestomathy. 1879. Square 8vo, cloth. 7s.

Socin (A.) Arabic Grammar. Paradigms, Literature, Chrestomathy and Glossary. By Dr. A. Socin, Professor, Tübingen. Crown 8vo, cloth. 7s. 6d.

Bopp's Comparative Grammar of the Sanscrit, Zend, Greek, Latin, Lithuanian, Gothic, German and Slavonic Languages. Translated by E. B. Eastwick. 4th Edition. 3 vols. 8vo, cloth. 31s. 6d.

Nestle (E.) Syriac Grammar. Literature, Chrestomathy and Glossary. By Professor E. Nestle, Professor, Tübingen. Translated into English. Crown 8vo, cloth. 9s.

Delitzsch (F.) Assyrian Grammar, with Paradigms, Exercises, Glossary and Bibliography. By Dr. F. Delitzsch. Translated into English by Prof. A. R. S. Kennedy, B.D. Crown 8vo, cloth. 15s.

Williams and Norgate's School Books and Maps.

Williams (T. S.) Modern German and English Conversations and Elementary Phrases, the German revised and corrected by A. Kokemueller. 21st enlarged and improved Edition. 12mo. cloth 3s

Williams (T. S.) and C. Cruse. German and English Commercial Correspondence. A Collection of Modern Mercantile Letters in German and English, with their Translation on opposite pages. 2nd Edition. 12mo. cloth 4s 6d

Apel (H.) German Prose Stories for Beginners (including Lessing's Prose Fables), with an interlinear Translation in the natural order of Construction. 2nd Edition. 12mo. cloth 2s 6d

———— **German Prose.** A Collection of the best Specimens of German Prose, chiefly from Modern Authors. A Handbook for Schools and Families. 500 pp. Crown 8vo. cloth 3s

German Classics for English Schools, with Notes and Vocabulary. Crown 8vo. cloth.

Schiller's Lied von der Glocke (The Song of the Bell), and other Poems and Ballads, by M. Förster 2s
———— Minor Poems. By Arthur P. Vernon 2s
———— Maria Stuart, by Moritz Förster 2s 6d
Goethe's Hermann und Dorothea, by M. Förster 2s 6d
———— Iphigenie auf Tauris. With Notes by H. Attwell. 2s
———— Egmont. By H. Apel 2s 6d
Lessing's Minna von Barnhelm, by Schmidt 2s 6d
———— Emilia Galotti. By G. Hein 2s
Chamisso's Peter Schlemihl, by M. Förster 2s
Andersen (H. C.) Bilderbuch ohne Bilder, by Beck 2s
Nieritz. Die Waise, a Tale, by Otte 2s
Hauff's Mærchen. A Selection, by A. Hoare 3s 6d

———

Carové (J. W.) Mæhrchen ohne Ende (The Story without an End). 12mo. cloth 2s
Fouque's Undine, Sintram, Aslauga's Ritter, die beiden Hauptleute. 4 vols. in 1. 8vo. cloth 7s 6d
  Undine. 1s 6d; cloth, 2s. Aslauga. 1s 6d; cloth, 2s
  Sintram. 2s 6d; cloth, 3s. Hauptleute. 1s 6d; cloth, 2s

Williams and Norgate's School Books and Maps.

Latin, Greek, etc.

Cæsar de Bello Gallico. Lib. I. Edited with Introduction, Notes and Maps, by ALEXANDER M. BELL, M.A. Ball. Coll., Oxon. Crown 8vo. cloth　　2s 6d

Euripides' Medea. The Greek Text, with Introduction and Explanatory Notes for Schools, by J. H. Hogan. 8vo. cloth　　3s 6d

―――― **Ion.** Greek Text, with Notes for Beginners, Introduction and Questions for Examination, by the Rev. Charles Badham, D.D. 2nd Edition. 8vo. 3s 6d

Æschylus. Agamemnon. Revised Greek Text, with literal line-for-line Translation on opposite pages, by John F. Davies, B.A. 8vo. cloth　　3s

Platonis Philebus. With Introduction and Notes by Dr. C. Badham. 2nd Edition, considerably augmented. 8vo. cloth　　4s

―――― **Euthydemus et Laches.** With Critical Notes, by the Rev. Ch. Badham, D.D. 8vo. cloth　　4s

―――― **Convivium,** cum Epistola ad Thompsonum, "De Platonis Legibus," edidit C. Badham. 8vo. cloth　4s

Dr. D. Zompolides. A Course of Modern Greek, or the Greek Language of the Present Day. I. The Elementary Method. Crown 8vo.　　5s

Kiepert New Atlas Antiquus. Maps of the Ancient World, for Schools and Colleges. 6th Edition. With a complete Geographical Index. Folio, boards　　7s 6d

Kampen. 15 Maps to illustrate Cæsar's De Bello Gallico. 15 coloured Maps. 4to. cloth　　3s 6d

Italian.

Volpe (Cav. G.) Eton Italian Grammar, for the use of Eton College. Including Exercises and Examples. New Edition. Crown 8vo. cloth (Key, 1s)　　4s 6d

Racconti Istorici e Novelle Morali. Edited, for the use of Italian Students, by G. Christison. 12th Edition. 18mo. cloth　　1s 6d

Rossetti. Exercises for securing Idiomatic Italian, by means of Literal Translations from the English by Maria F. Rossetti. 12mo. cloth　　3s 6d

―――― **Aneddoti Italiani.** One Hundred Italian Anecdotes, selected from "Il Compagno del Passeggio."

Williams and Norgate's School Books and Maps.

Being also a Key to Rossetti's Exercises. 12mo. cloth 2s 6d
Venosta (F.) Raccolta di Poesie. Crown 8vo. cloth 5s

Wall Maps.

Sydow's Wall Maps of Physical Geography for Schoolrooms, representing the purely physical proportions of the Globe. An English Edition, the Originals with English Names and Explanations.
Mounted on canvas, with rollers : each 10s
1. The World; 2. Europe; 3. Asia; 4. Africa; 5. America; (North and South) ; 6. Australia and Australasia.
—— Handbook to the Series of Large Physical Maps for School Instruction, edited by J. Tilleard. 8vo. 1s

Miscellaneous.

Fyfe (W. T.) First Lessons in Rhetoric. With Exercises. By W. T. FYFE, M.A., Senior English Master, High School for Girls, Aberdeen. 12mo. 1s
Reiff's Russian Grammar for Englishmen. 4th Edition, cloth 6s
De Rheims (H.) Practical Lines in Geometrical Drawing, containing the Use of Mathematical Instruments and the Construction of Scales, illustrated with 300 Diagrams, 8vo. cloth 9s
Hebrew Texts. Large type. 4 vols. 16mo. cloth. 1 Genesis ; 2 Psalms ; 3 Job ; 4 Isaiah. each 1s
Hebrew Grammar, with Exercises, Paradigms, Chrestomathy and Glossary. By Professor H. STRACK, D.D., of Berlin. Crown 8vo. cloth 4s 6d
Arabic Grammar. Paradigms, Literature, Chrestomathy and Glossary. By Dr. A. SOCIN, Professor, Tübingen. Translated into English. Crown 8vo. cloth 7s 6d
Attwell (Prof. H.) Table of Aryan (Indo-European) Languages, showing their Classification and Affinities, with copious Notes; to which is added Grimm's Law of the Interchange of Mute Consonants, with numerous Illustrations. A **Wall Map** for the use of Colleges and Lecture-rooms. 2nd Edition. Mounted with rollers 10s
—— The same Table, in 4to. with numerous Additions. Boards 7s 6d

www.ingramcontent.com/pod-product-compliance
Lightning Source LLC
Chambersburg PA
CBHW030436190426
43202CB00036B/1357